Dedicated to parents,
the primary power
in the prevention of drug abuse

Contents

Appreciations

For all they have taught us, we want to thank our many teachers, colleagues, and mentors in the field of chemical dependency and prevention, especially those at the University of Minnesota, Minneapolis Community College, and Project Charlie. We also thank the children and parents in the Minnesota public schools and the families we have known in recovery programs.

Thanks especially to Dr. Peter Benson for his encouragement and support and to Jim Epperly for his assistance in collecting research data from elementary students.

For love, joy, laughter, and for keeping us honest, we thank our families: Chuck, Paul, Ann, Andrew, and Charlie Gesme, Diane Jarvenpa, Jim Epperly, Sam London Epperly, and Dick, Marc, Jennifer, and Wade Clarke.

We thank the people who read the manuscript for this book and shared their thoughtful responses with us: Scott Davis, Jerry Jaker, David Schreiber, Betsy Arnow, Joy Wander, Ginger Kauppi, RoAnne Elliott, Sue Blaszczak, Peter Benson, Christine Ternand, Jon and Laurie Weiss, Bernie Saunders, Nat Houtz, Mary Paananen, Teresa Kamrath, Lonnie Bell, Patsy Martin, Pamela L. Searles, Eva Lockhart, Mahri Monson, and Adam Lawrence.

We also thank the many people who contributed to the Suggestion Circles, including Drew Betz, Darlene Montz and the Mount Olivet Lutheran High School class of Yakima, Washington, Barbara Beystrom, Susan Clarke, Julie Foley, Midge Lockovitch, Margaret Matzko, Pat Miller, Denise Mitten, Lynnell Thiel, Chas Wilson, Kao Yang, Mai Vang, Kay

Joppru, Ramona Oswald, Beth Brekke, Kathryn Hammerseng, Patty Gardner, Joan Baraf, Maggie Lawrence, Athalie Terry, Dick Clarke, and Charles Gesme.

We appreciate you all.

What Is This Book About?
Preventing Drug Abuse

Cutting off the demand is the only way to stop drug use and abuse. Forget border patrols! There are no borders! Every tiny airfield, every flat field large enough to accommodate a small plane is a border. Every window box, flower pot, and backyard garden is a border.

Forget asking other countries to stop producing drugs. Consider a campesino living in the Andes. He makes a marginal living farming. He is approached by a pair of strangers who say, "Here is free seed. Plant this instead of potatoes. We'll be back at harvest time and pay you ten times the price of potatoes. Oh, and by the way, if you don't we'll kill you." Is the farmer going to say, "Oh, no thank you. Keep your free seed. Cocaine might put American children at risk"?

This book is about preventing drug abuse before it begins and about preventing more or further drug abuse. It is about the parent's role in prevention—the role researchers now assure us is more powerful than peer pressure.

It is about

- what to do instead of drugs

- what to teach by daily living

- what to teach directly

- what to know about drugs

- misinformation and myths about the power of the parents and the family versus peer group pressure.

It is about the difference any parent can make by being a powerful agent in drug abuse prevention.

It is also about preventing violence and other delinquent behavior.

It is about how you can celebrate what you are doing now as a family and change what you need to change.

How to Use This Book

- Do use it in the way that helps you.

- Do pay attention to the drug abuse prevention keys. You can work on them one at a time.

- Do think about each item you read.

- Do use the Suggestion Circle ideas to help you. Suggestion Circles were collected from parents in many places and contain the wisdom of people from many different kinds of families. We have thanked the person who collected the ideas or the person who asked for the circle. Sometimes the solutions sound contradictory. Think about whether one of the solutions would work in your family. Or you can lead your own circle (see page 149).

- Do use the activities as often as you need to.

- Do learn how drugs affect the body and how drugs differ.

- Do believe in your own ability and trust yourself.

- Don't expect simple answers or pat formulas. Raising children is more complex than that.

- Don't shame yourself if you aren't perfect. No one is. Children don't need perfect parents, they need parents who do things well enough.

- Don't get stuck in the past. Move ahead.

- Don't fault yourself if you didn't know how important your role is. For years parents have been invited to feel powerless in the face of peer pressure. This book offers hope that you can make a profound difference with lots of suggestions about how to do that.

- Don't withdraw into the family as the only source of help for children. Reach out to others who support and value living a drug-free life.

Twenty-Four Keys to Drug Abuse Prevention

The following twenty-four keys can be used as guidelines to halt drug abuse before it starts or to help families change direction if someone has already been using alcohol or other drugs. Start with the one you are most likely to succeed at. Practice and explore it. Then add others. First, let's define each key briefly. Later we'll discuss them in depth.

Key 1: Provide Love and Structure

The love and consistent structure that parents offer is the first line of defense against alcohol and other drug abuse.

Key 2: Build Self-Esteem

It is important for parents to encourage, reward, and celebrate self-esteem in their children and in themselves.

Key 3: Affirm Each Stage of Growth

Every age is a good age at which to remind your children of their right to be healthy and to enjoy life without using drugs.

Key 4: Teach Values

The family is the hearth at which values are forged. Parents teach their values by words and deeds.

Key 5: Be an Active Role Model About Drug Use

Children need to see responsible attitudes and behavior concerning drug use in their most important role models, their parents.

Key 6: Talk About Drugs

Children want their parents to initiate talking knowledgeably about alcohol and other drugs and their effects.

Key 7: Value Drug-Free Celebrations

Learning ways to celebrate, play, and have fun without the aid of alcohol or other drugs is an important deterrent to drug abuse because it models healthy choices.

Key 8: Cherish Rituals and Traditions

As parents we need to realize that tradition and rituals are part of the consistent structure that gives stability to children's lives. It is our job to create rituals and traditions that are meaningful for every family member.

Key 9: Promote Spiritual Growth

Children need guidance in their spiritual growth.

Key 10: Teach Empathy

Not only do children need to be helped to understand that caring about others is important, but they need to learn how by helping their parents care for others.

Key 11: Resolve Grief

Children need the family to be a safe place for them to mourn the many losses they encounter while growing up.

Key 12: Practice Delayed Gratification

The degree of freedom children will experience as adults may depend partly on how they learn to defer the urge to "have it all" now.

Key 13: Share History of Drug Use, Abuse, or Addiction in the Family

Children deserve to know that they are more likely to develop alcohol or other drug problems if there is a history of these problems among family members.

Key 14: Make Decisions, Plan for Action

It is important for children to know how to make decisions and solve problems before they are confronted with pressures to use drugs.

Key 15: Respect Feelings

It is our job as parents to teach and model for children how to accept, understand, label, and appropriately express feelings.

Key 16: Resist Negative Peer Pressure

Resisting peer pressure is a skill that allows children to make their own decisions about their behavior. The parents' job is to teach children this skill.

Key 17: Support Positive Peer Pressure

Children need to learn how to make and maintain healthy friendships.

Key 18: Practice Positive Communication Skills

Children need to practice effective communication skills—both speaking and listening—within the family.

Key 19: Resist Media Messages

The media send constant, persuasive messages that drug abuse is OK. Children deserve to know how to recognize and resist those messages.

Key 20: Learn About Drugs, Needles, AIDS, and Sex

AIDS has added a whole new fatal aspect to drug abuse.

Key 21: Connect with Community

Children need to understand the importance of their membership in several communities, including family, school, neighborhood, nation, and humanity.

Key 22: Encourage Adult Support

Grade school–age children and adolescents need at least three adults outside of their families to ask for help. The teenager, to help form an identity and expand values, needs to have frequent, serious conversations with an adult who is not his or her parent.

Key 23: Get Involved with School

Children need to feel connected with school and to have positive experiences socially and academically. Parents need to be directly involved in the school.

Key 24: Be Informed About Drugs

In order to be credible and reliable resources for their children, parents need to know about the effects of different drugs on the mind and the body.

These keys are not arranged in order of importance, and the length of each key section will not imply how important that key is for your family. That will vary from family to family.

Preventing drug abuse is a complex problem. You can think of it as a door with twenty-four locks. You probably have many of the keys already.

Calvin and Hobbes   **by Bill Watterson**

Key 1: Provide Love and Structure

*The love and consistent structure that parents offer
is the first line of defense against alcohol
or other drug abuse.*

Is peer pressure the major cause of drug abuse? No. We can let that myth go. There are many causes, and the major deterrent to drug or alcohol abuse is found in the personal values that are fostered in the family. (See Search, *The Troubled Journey.*)

This is great news! After all, parents can't control all that goes on in a peer group, but they have great power to make the family a safe and supportive place for children.

What do children need? They need love. Lots of it. They need a parent who has some understanding of developmental tasks. They need a parent who is committed to them (Stinnett, DeFrain), who cares enough not to let them watch unlimited TV, not to let them spend four evenings a week hanging out with friends, not to overindulge them with too much money or too few rules. They need a parent who will teach strong values, who involves the children in family activities, who insists that children do homework, who prepares them for the risks that teenagers inevitably take by supplying accurate information about alcohol, drugs, and sex, and by teaching them when delayed gratification is valuable.

They need structure—the rules that protect them and the skills that will let them be competent. You can look at the Suggestion Circle that follows for other parents' ideas about structure. Then you can use the Asset Checklists to take stock of your strengths and pick one area you want to improve. You can make a difference!

Suggestion Circle

I'm shocked to learn from a national study that 31 percent of students from sixth grade through high school attend drinking parties at a friend's house (See Search). What can I do to protect my children?

Think about these ideas and decide what you will do.

- Call the parents to find out if they are serving drinks. If they are, help your children plan other activities.

- Make sure it doesn't happen at your house.

- Talk with other parents about your alarm. Let your children see that you are taking action because this is not OK for kids.

- Teach children how to say no and how to say yes. Model that for them.

- Join or form a parent network so you know your children's friends and their parents.

- Keep a family notebook where everyone, including parents, writes where he or she is going and what time he or she will be home.

- See to it that your children are involved in supervised community, church, or temple activities.

- I'd teach them how to have fun without alcohol.

- Make sure you know who they are going with, whose home they will be at, and whether or not parents will be at home.

Thanks to Sandra Sittko, Eagan, MN

Activity—An Asset Checklist for Teens and Parents

*Assets are factors promoting positive teenage develop-
ment. These assets may result from "external" factors
such as positive relationships in families, friendship
groups, schools, and the community, or they may result
from "internal" factors reflecting the teenager's personal convictions, values, and attitudes.*

This checklist was used with teens by Search Institute. The
authors recommend that you also use the checklist with
younger children.

Use M for mostly, S for sometimes, N for not often enough.
Parents and children fill out the checklist separately and then
compare answers.

Teens	Parents	How many external assets are present in the teen's life?
_____	_____	Parents are loving, easy to talk to and available when teens want to talk.
_____	_____	Parents frequently take time to talk seriously with their children.
_____	_____	Parents express their own standards for teenage behavior.
_____	_____	Parents talk with their teenager about school and sometimes help with school work and attend school events.
_____	_____	Parents set rules and enforce the consequences when the rules are broken.
_____	_____	Parents check on where their teenager is going, with whom, and for how long.
_____	_____	Parents are approachable when the teenager has something serious to talk about.

(continued)

Teens	Parents	How many external assets are present in the teen's life?
_____	_____	The number of nights the teenager may spend out of the home "for fun and recreation" is limited.
_____	_____	The teenager has three or more adults, in addition to parents, to whom he or she could go for help.
_____	_____	The teenager has frequent serious conversations with an adult who is not his or her own parent.
_____	_____	The teenager's friends are a constructive influence, are doing well at school, are staying away from contact with drugs, alcohol, and other at-risk behavior.
_____	_____	The teenager attends church or synagogue at least once a month.
_____	_____	The teenager sees the school atmosphere as caring and encouraging.
_____	_____	The teenager participates in band, orchestra, or takes lessons on a musical instrument involving three or more hours of practice a week.
_____	_____	The teenager participates in school sports activities or other organizations three or more hours a week.
_____	_____	The teenager participates in non-school-sponsored sports or other organizations three or more hours per week.

Teens	Parents	*How many internal assets are present in the teen's life?*
_____	_____	The teenager tries to do his or her best at school.
_____	_____	Hopes to be educated beyond high school.
_____	_____	Earns above-average school grades.
_____	_____	Does six or more hours of homework weekly.
_____	_____	Is good at making friends.
_____	_____	Tries to stand up for her or his beliefs.
_____	_____	Cares about others' feelings.
_____	_____	Is good at planning ahead.
_____	_____	Is good at making decisions.
_____	_____	Has a positive attitude toward self.
_____	_____	Envisions a happy future for herself or himself.
_____	_____	Shows concern for others, including the poor and the homeless.
_____	_____	Is interested in helping and improving life for others.
_____	_____	Holds values that prohibit having sex as a teenager.

According to Dr. Peter Benson, young people ideally should have at least twenty-five of the thirty assets listed above. The average young person has about sixteen out of thirty.

Information from Search Institute, The Troubled Journey: A Portrait of 6th–12th Grade Youth, *by Dr. Peter L. Benson.*

Assets—Help to Prevent Alcohol and Drug Abuse

The numbers below are percentages of youth who reported having the assets.

List of Assets

External

1. Parental monitoring (77 percent)
2. Parental standards (75 percent)
3. Time at home (70 percent)
4. Involved in school extracurricular activities (62 percent)
5. Parental discipline (60 percent)
6. Involved in church or synagogue (57 percent)
7. Family support (56 percent)
8. Other adult resources (49 percent)
9. Parent communication (48 percent)
10. Parent(s) as social resources (45 percent)

Internal

1. Cares about people's feelings (88 percent)
2. Educational aspiration (86 percent)
3. Assertiveness skills (82 percent)
4. Friendship-making skills (74 percent)
5. Decision-making skills (74 percent)
6. Achievement motivation (72 percent)
7. Positive view of personal future (68 percent)
8. Planning skills (57 percent)
9. Values helping people (48 percent)
10. Satisfactory school performance (46 percent)

11. Other adult communica-   11. Self-esteem
    tion (42 percent)   (45 percent)

12. Involved in community   12. Concerned about world
    organizations or activities   hunger (43 percent)
    (39 percent)

13. Positive school climate   13. Values sexual restraint
    (30 percent)   (35 percent)

14. Positive peer influence   14. Does homework
    (30 percent)   (26 percent)

15. Involved in music
    (27 percent)

16. Parent involvement in
    schooling (26 percent)

Information from Search Institute, The Troubled Journey: A
Portrait of 6th–12th Grade Youth, *by Dr. Peter L. Benson.*

Deficits

Now let's look at the percentage of families in the Search
Institute research that have the deficit factors.

As defined in the study, "Deficits are factors *inhibiting*
healthy teenage development. They include influences which
limit access to external assets, which block development of internal assets, or which ease the way into risky behavioral
choices including drug abuse. Deficits are liabilities, none of
which necessarily does permanent harm, but each of which
makes harm more probable." Numbers are percentages of
youth who reported having the deficits.

List of Deficits

1. Alone at home (58 percent)
   Student spends two or more hours per day at home without an adult.

2. Hedonistic values (48 percent)
   Student places high importance on self-serving values.

3. TV overexposure (40 percent)
   Student watches TV three or more hours per day.

4. Drinking parties (31 percent)
   Student frequently attends parties where peers drink.

5. Stress (21 percent)
   Student feels under stress or pressure "most" or "all" of the time.

6. Physical abuse (17 percent)
   Student reports at least one incident of physical abuse by an adult.

7. Sexual abuse (10 percent)
   Student reports at least one incident of sexual abuse.

8. Parental addiction (7 percent)
   Student reports a parent "has a serious problem with alcohol or drugs."

9. Social isolation (6 percent)
   Student feels a consistent lack of care, support, and understanding.

10. Negative peer pressure (2 percent)
    Most close friends are involved in chemical use and/or are in frequent trouble at school.

11. Being raised in poverty.

A total of 8 percent reported none of the deficits.

Information from Search Institute, The Troubled Journey: A Portrait of 6th–12th Grade Youth, *by Dr. Peter L. Benson*

Signs of Alcohol or Other Drug Abuse

Behavioral Signs of an Adolescent Who May Be Abusing Alcohol or Other Drugs

Parents need to know the signs of alcohol/drug abuse.

Many of the behaviors listed below are normal expressions of adolescent growth. Be aware of extremes, which may indicate a need for serious concern. Also watch for clusters of clues. Before coming to any conclusions, consult your school counselor or a drug/alcohol counselor.

1. A drop in grades
2. Switching friends
3. Emotional highs and lows
4. Defiance of rules and regulations
5. Becoming more secretive
6. Loss of initiative
7. Withdrawing from family functions
8. Change in physical hygiene
9. Not informing you of school activities
10. Many excuses for staying out late
11. Isolating themselves
12. Suspicion of money or alcohol missing
13. Selling possessions
14. Parents feeling manipulated and bargained with
15. Weight changes
16. Short-tempered
17. Legal problems
18. Becoming more defensive

19. Cues from the school about problem behavior
20. Coming home drunk or high
21. Abusive behavior toward others
22. Unfamiliar odors (incense, marijuana)
23. Lying or manipulating the truth

Information from Horizons Summit Center, 6 Hospital Plaza, Clarksburg, WV 26301 (phone: 1-304-623-5661)

Key 2: Build Self-Esteem

It is important for parents to encourage, reward, and celebrate self-esteem in their children and in themselves.

Self-esteem is a deep, private, inner quality. It is self-love in the biblical sense:"Thou shalt love thy neighbor as thyself." It is the fine balance of believing that we are both lovable and capable, feeling that way, and behaving in ways that are respectful to ourselves and to other people. It is true humility. It determines the extent to which we allow ourselves to be successful, and to be loved, lovable, and loving. It would be hard for someone who truly esteemed himself to harm himself with drugs.

Self-esteem is built slowly and needs to be maintained daily. Since self-esteem is an internal quality, it is the personal responsibility of each individual and cannot be "given" to our children, no matter how much we parents would like to be able to do that. Parents are responsible for the process; children are responsible for the results.

Parents do, however, offer some of the elements from which children decide their own self-image. Children's fates are their own; their decisions are also theirs. Beyond that, parents can offer a great deal—affirmations, the safety of love, a protected environment, the security of rules, clear communication, family rituals, spiritual values, and healthy role modeling. Parents can also offer challenges when they see children behaving in ways that indicate that they are making poor decisions.

You can use the affirmations (page 23–27) to help you express love in supportive ways. Remember that you, the parent, are in charge of the rules in your family as you look at what other parents do in the Suggestion Circles that follow.

You can read more about self-esteem in Clarke's Self-Esteem: A Family Affair.

Suggestion Circle

Parents' consistent limit setting is one step toward building self-esteem and preventing drug abuse.

We have set some limits for our teenagers, and it seems like their friends have no rules. What should we do?

Think about these ideas and decide what you will do.

- Be reasonable—but stick to your rules.

- Be clear that you have and enforce rules because your children are important to you.

- Tell your kids that it is the parents' job to set the rules and the kids' job to follow them, and they don't have to enjoy it.

- Make contracts with your teenagers and see that they keep the contracts no matter what their friends do.

- If friends are doing things that are not safe, restrict the friendship.

- Tell stories about what happens when there is structure and when there is no structure. Read *Growing Up Again* by Clarke and Dawson.

- Be sure your kids know the difference between rules they can help decide and rules that for safety's sake are non-negotiable.

- Say, "All kids deserve to have parents who care enough to be in charge of the family rules. I'm sorry your friends don't have that."

Thanks to Dick Clarke, Eden Prairie, MN

Key 3: Affirm Each Stage of Growth

*Every age is a good age at which to remind
your children of their right to be healthy
and to enjoy life without using drugs.*

Children long for and need affirmation from their parents. Affirmations are all the things parents do and say that let children know they are lovable and capable. The affirmations presented here are helpful to us all of our lives.

We've grouped the affirmations by sets of developmental tasks and by the ages at which they first become focus tasks for children. Use the messages to remind you what children need to be deciding and what you need to be offering at different ages. If you find messages that you didn't give or that a child doesn't believe, give them now. Learn to believe the affirmations as you give them. Otherwise you offer conflicting messages that confuse children. Give the affirmations to your children regularly by word and deed, and teach your children to give them to you.

The research on successful families (Stinnett, DeFrain) indicates that those families have lots of positive communication and a high degree of commitment. Here are some ways to express that.

Being
—Birth to six months and ever after—

I'm glad
you are
alive.

You
belong
here.

What you
need is
important
to me.

I'm glad
you are
you.

You can
grow at your
own pace.

You can
feel all
of your
feelings.

I love you
and I care
for you
willingly.

Copy these ovals and color them red.
Post them for daily reading.

Being—the Right to Exist

An important emotional and social task of infants is to learn to trust, to decide to be. They need to experience and to be sure that it is all right for them to live, to be who they are, to have needs, and to find ways to get those needs met.

Young people who don't believe in their right to exist may turn to drugs to ease the pain.

Doing—the Right to Be Active, to Initiate, and to Explore

During the toddler stage children explore their environment and learn to trust their senses. They investigate their world in order to develop their intelligence, their sense of self, and their ability to do things.

Young people who feel stifled, emotionally dead, or inadequate to reach out and meet life may turn to drugs to ease the pain.

Doing
—Six to eighteen months and ever after—

You can explore and experiment and I will support and protect you.

You can use all of your senses when you explore.

You can do things as many times as you need to.

You can know what you know.

You can be interested in everything.

I like to watch you initiate and grow and learn.

I love you when you are active and when you are quiet.

Copy these ovals and color them orange.
Post them for daily reading.

Copyright © Jean Illsley Clarke

Thinking—the Right to Think and to Feel Independently of Others

Here are some special affirming messages that will help children during the two-year-old stage, when they need to become separate, learn to think for themselves, explore anger and resistance, and learn cause-and-effect thinking.

Young people who don't believe that their thoughts and feelings count may turn to drugs to ease the pain.

Identity and Power—the Right to Be Who You Are, to Exert Your Power to Get Your Needs Met, and to Help Others

During the preschool years, children are exploring their identities and ways of being powerful, acquiring lots of information, starting to learn socially appropriate behavior, developing their imaginations, and trying out different ways of

Thinking
—Eighteen months to three years and ever after—

I'm glad you are thinking for yourself.

It's OK for you to be angry and I won't let you hurt yourself or others.

You can say no and push and test limits as much as you need to.

You can learn to think for yourself and I will think for myself.

You can think and feel at the same time.

You can know what you need and ask for help.

You can become separate from me and I will continue to love you.

Copy these ovals and color them yellow.
Post them for daily reading.

Identity and Power
—Three to six years and ever after—

You can explore who you are and find out who other people are.

You can be powerful and ask for help at the same time.

You can try out different roles and ways of being powerful.

You can find out the results of your behavior.

All of your feelings are OK with me.

You can learn what is pretend and what is real.

I love who you are.

Copy these ovals and color them green.
Post them for daily reading.

relating to other people.

Young people who don't believe that their uniqueness is acceptable or that they have the ability to shape their world may turn to drugs to ease the pain.

Structure—the Right to Learn Skills, to Become Competent, and to Set and Defend Boundaries

During the grade school years, children are developing their own structures, competence, and values, and are learning about other people's rules, their own rules, and the relevance of rules.

Young people who have not internalized good rules about their health and well-being and about their ability to set limits and still be accepted may turn to drugs to ease the pain.

Identity, Sexuality, and Separation—the Right to Explore a Unique Identity, Expand a Personal Value Base, Accept Sexuality, and Prepare for Adult Responsibilities and Privileges

These affirming messages help young people achieve the tasks of adolescence. You give these affirmations by the way you

- affirm or challenge your child's values

- interact with your adolescent

- respond to his or her sometimes dramatic changes in mood and interests that will increase as he or she recycles earlier developmental tasks now that sexuality is an important part of growth

- affirm your child's emerging sexuality without being seductive

- support his or her emotional separation first

- support physical separation later

Structure
—Six to twelve years and ever after—

You can think before you say yes or no and learn from your mistakes.

You can trust your intuition to help you decide what to do.

You can find a way of doing things that works for you.

You can learn the rules that help you live with others.

You can learn when and how to disagree.

You can think for yourself and get help instead of staying in distress.

I love you even when we differ; I love growing with you.

**Copy these ovals and color them light blue.
Post them for daily reading.**

Identity, Sexuality, Separation
—Teenage years and ever after—

You can know who you are and learn and practice skills for independence.

You can learn the difference between sex and nurturing and be responsible for your needs and behavior.

You can develop your own interests, relationships, and causes.

You can learn to use old skills in new ways.

You can grow in your maleness or femaleness and still be dependent at times.

I look forward to knowing you as an adult.

My love is always with you. I trust you to ask for my support.

**Copy these ovals and color them dark blue.
Post them for daily reading.**

- (or) support his or her growing independence while he or she continues to live at home.

Young people who do not believe that their uniqueness is important, that their sexuality is acceptable, that they can build satisfactory relationships, that they can delay gratification, or that they can make a difference in their world may turn to drugs to ease the pain.

Interdependence—the Right to Become an Autonomous Adult Among Adults, to Care for Others and Be Cared for, to Make a Contribution to the World

The developmental tasks of adulthood focus on the journey from dependence through independence to interdependence and include regular recycling of earlier tasks in ways that support the specific adult tasks.

Young adults who have low self-esteem, who do not feel competent to become independent, to take on adult roles and make their contributions, to form lasting and intimate relationships, to care for a younger and an older generation, to handle adult stresses, and to face the many changes of the long adult years, may turn to drugs to ease the pain.

You can learn more about the affirmations,
about developmental tasks at each age,
and about recycling by reading
Clarke's Self-Esteem: A Family Affair;
Growing Up Again, *by Clarke and Dawson;*
the first two books in the Help! For Parents *series, by Clarke et al.;*
and Becoming the Way We Are, *by Pamela Levin.*

Interdependence
—Adults—

Your
needs
are
important.

You can be
uniquely
yourself and
honor the
uniqueness
of others.

You can be
independent
and
interdependent.

You can be
creative,
competent,
productive,
and joyful.

You can
trust your
inner
wisdom.

You can say
your hellos and
good-byes to
people, roles,
dreams, and
decisions.

Through the years
you can expand your
commitments to your
own growth, to your
family, your friends,
your community, and
to all humankind.

You can build
and examine your
commitments to
your values and
causes, your
roles and your
tasks.

You can be
responsible
for your
contributions to
each of your
commitments.

You can finish
each part of
your journey and
look forward to
the next.

Your love
matures
and
expands.

You are
lovable
at
every age.

**Copy these ovals and color them lilac or purple.
Post them for daily reading.**

Key 4: Teach Values

The family is the hearth at which values are forged.
Parents teach their values by words and deeds.

People make decisions based on their values. The internal assets that promote drug-free development of teenagers, listed on page 14, are all reflections of values.

Parents offer their values by word and by deed. Young people then claim their own values and develop their own ideals.

Families teach values directly when they attend places of worship, proclaim beliefs, and join with others to take action based on their values.

Parents also teach about values informally at every age. They ask the young child: "How did you feel when that boy wouldn't help you? What are some ways you help other people?" They ask the older child: "What do you think of kids who cheat? Do you ever want to cheat? How do you keep yourself from cheating?" They let the children hear the adults discussing their own or other adults' abstinence, drug use, or drug abuse, and ask the children what they think.

Young people who said they did not know how their parents would react, or said that their parents wouldn't mind if they found out the young people were drinking, were much more likely to be involved with alcohol and other drugs than those who said their parents would be extremely upset. Some young people try using drugs out of curiosity. **Strong parental disapproval if a child has used drugs is an important deterrent to further use.** So feel free to yell about drugs. (MSSR)

Look at the Suggestion Circles and think about what you

would do and on what values you based your decisions. Use the Activities in this book to help you sort your values.

Suggestion Circle

When my nine-year-old asks, "What's the purpose of life, what's important?" how should I answer?

(Yes, an actual nine-year-old did ask this very real question.) Think about these ideas and decide what you would do.

- Say, "You know me and what I do. What do you think my values are?"

- Tell your nine-year-old, "I'm glad you are thinking about that." Ask, "What is important to you right now?"

- Happiness is the result of striving for and reaching different goals at different ages.

- Say, "I think the purpose of life is to leave the world a better place because I was here. What would you most like people to say about you when you are grown-up?"

- To do the best you can with what you have.

- To be the best person you can be and to help other people.

- Ask her to recite the Golden Rule, "Do onto others as you would have them do onto you."

- To believe in God and to celebrate life.

- Say, "To be committed to something. Do you know what that means?"

- To be responsible.

- To learn how to love. "Love the answer is no matter what the question is."

Thanks to Mary Paananen, Seattle, WA

Discounting

Discounting is the process of treating something as if it were less or different than it really is. Parental discounting or denying increases the probability that children will be confused about drugs.

Sometimes when parents think about how important it is to teach values and how powerful their influence and way of life are for a child, they wish these things weren't so. And they try denying their role. They say:

1. "Well, drugs won't be a problem with our kids."

or

2. "It's not a big problem in our neighborhood."

or

3. "The experts don't agree on how to prevent drug abuse, so why try?"

or

4. "I don't know what to do."

Remember, if you discount or fail to take action for any of the four following reasons, the problem does not get solved.

1. There is no problem.

2. This problem is not serious.

3. Nobody knows how to solve this.

4. I don't know what to do.

Instead of discounting, ask the *empowering* questions:

1. What is the problem?

2. How serious is it?

3. How have others dealt with this problem?

4. What shall I do?

and then

5. Do it.

You can read more about discounting in Clarke and Dawson's Growing Up Again.

Suggestion Circle

What can I do when I'm with parents who buy drinks for underage children in bars and restaurants? I don't approve.

Think about these ideas and decide what you will do.

- Let it go, but later let your children know that it is not OK in your family.

- Make a statement to the whole group about how you feel and your concerns about underage drinking.

- Remind the parents that it's against the law.

- Let the waiter know that there are young people at the table who are not of drinking age.

- Share information about prevention and drug use with these parents at a separate occasion when they are without their children.

- Tell these parents that you cannot in good conscience have future dinners with them if they are encouraging their children to drink.

Thanks to Larry Peterson, Red Wing, MN

Beware of People Who Discount and Act Powerless

No problem. "They are with their parent, so it's not a problem. One or two drinks won't hurt."

Not serious. "I'd rather see kids drinking with their parents than with their peers."

No solution. "You can't stop parents from doing what they want to with their children."

No personal power. "Nothing I can do. I might lose their friendship."

Empowered action. Read the Suggestion Circles again. What would you do?

Activity—Values and Attitudes About Drug Use

Everyone holds values about drug use. Rank order the following examples of drug use from 1 (least damaging) to 15 (most damaging). If this task is difficult, remember that the object is to stimulate thinking about your values. There is no right or wrong answer.

_____ A friend who gives neighborhood youngsters caffeinated soft drinks.

_____ The coach who looks the other way when his players put on a lot of muscle from obvious steroid use.

_____ The doctor who prescribes Valium or Xanax for every complaint of stress.

_____ The child-care worker who gives decongestants to children without their parents' knowledge.

_____ The parent who offers teenagers their choice of wine coolers or soft drinks.

_____ The father who serves wine to family members, young and old, at holiday gatherings.

_____ Someone who discovers a marijuana plant in her backyard and leaves it there.

_____ An adult who uses a child as bartender.

_____ The boss who picks his inner circle based on who will go to happy hour with him.

_____ The friend who asks to share your prescription pain
pills.

_____ A person who drives after several drinks.

_____ Someone who gives a line of cocaine to a friend.

_____ An adult who allows a child to sip drinks.

Ask each family member to rank order this list. Compare
your answers, and talk about why you ranked the way you
did, not about who is right or wrong.

Key 5: Be an Active Role Model About Drug Use

Children need to see responsible attitudes and behavior concerning drug use in their most important role models, their parents.

Your Children Are Watching

"Children learn best by example" is parenting advice that has been around a long time.

Parents teach about drugs by the way they abstain from, use, or abuse them. There are four common ways families approach drinking.

Don't Drink	*Don't Drink*	*Drink*	*Abuse*
condemn those who do	advocate moderation	advocate and model moderation	use alcohol in harmful ways

Children will decide whether or not to use drugs, but parents are the most important influence on that decision (Brown U., pp. 191–200). There is no research that says parental drinking or use of medicines is harmful to children unless a parent is misusing or abusing these drugs.

If parents use drugs regularly without limits or standards, the children learn to do the same. If adults brag about overindulgence or laugh at others who are drunk or high, children learn that drug abuse is not only tolerated, it is approved.

Remember, you don't have to be a perfect role model in all aspects of parenting. Children get the big picture and forgive slips and mistakes. Do the best you can.

Suggestion Circle

In my family there was alcohol abuse. In my husband's family alcohol was the "tool of the devil." We occasionally drink moderately. What do we say when our teenager says, "You drink, why can't I?"

Think about these ideas and decide what you will do.

- Say, "We are the adults and we are making adult decisions. When you are an adult, I hope you will also make responsible decisions."

- Ask them if your drinking concerns them.

- Ask the children what they think about drinking alcohol.

- Stop using alcohol yourself.

- Say, "There are many things that adults can do that young people are not ready to do and this is one of them. Your liver is not fully able to break down alcohol until you are twenty-one to twenty-four years old."

- Say, "You can when you are legal age. We obey the law in our family."

- Say, "Your mind and body are still developing, and alcohol can only hurt you at this crucial stage in your life."

Thanks to Carole Gesme, Minnetonka, MN

Suggestion Circle

I grew up using drugs and used them in front of my children. What can I do about that now?

Think about these ideas and decide what you will do.

- Say, "What I did at that time was not helpful. I'd like our family to move forward now."

- I would explain the effect of the drugs and tell why it's not good for me.

- Tell them, "I made a mistake in my life, and I don't want you to make the same mistake I did."

- Using myself as an example, I would teach the child the harmful effects of drugs.

- Stop using drugs and get help and tell the child you are doing that.

- I'd talk about my natural consequence and the new family rule and the consequences for using drugs or alcohol.

- I would apologize to the children for exposing them to drugs.

- If you are drug free, say that it was clearly wrong and harmful to use and that you no longer use drugs.

- Say, "If only I knew then what I know now, I would never have done that. At least I've learned from the past."

Thanks to a member of a twelve-step program

Suggestion Circle

My partner is abusing drugs/alcohol in front of my children. What can I do about it?

Think about these ideas and decide what you will do.

- Get help for yourself such as the twelve-step program Alanon.

- Explain to your child that your partner needs help.

- Bring it up with the child as opposed to ignoring it. "This is the way Dad is doing it and this is the way I am doing it, and you must decide what you will do. I respect your dad in many ways, but here I feel Dad is on the wrong track."

- I love your father—but I don't like what he's doing.

- Ask for advice from a counselor or member of the clergy about how to handle this situation.

- Confront the abuser and set very strict limits. If the limits aren't followed, move yourself and your child out of the relationship.

- If your partner is unwilling to get help, figure out how to keep yourself and your child safe.

- Affirm your child and get help.

- Teach kids they didn't cause the alcohol or other drug abuse and they can't cure it. Teach coping skills.

- Confront the abuser and set very strict limits. If the limits aren't followed, I'd terminate the relationship.

Thanks to Ramona Oswald, Plymouth, MN

Activity—Deciding About Drugs

Read the following stories about family A and family B. After each paragraph, imagine what decisions about drugs three-year-old Ben, ten-year-old Samantha, and a child the age of yours might have made. If you notice some changes you would like to make after you read about these families, this book will help you make them.

Family A

The kids watched their mother carefully. They knew she was having a bad morning. She even told them not to bother her until she'd had her coffee. They watched her have the third cup, but they didn't see much change. Later she took one of her pills to settle her stomach. She said, "Pills make you feel better. Your dad and I had too much to drink at the party last night, but it was worth it. I had a good time."

Decisions the children might make about using drugs:

_____

_____

Family B

Mother B was having a bad morning. She asked the children to be quiet until after she'd had a cup of coffee. Then she asked the children if they wanted to join her in some exercises. She said, "I feel groggy this morning. I had some wine at dinner last night and I have a headache this morning. I'll think twice before I do that again. I like to have wine when your dad and I go out for dinner, but it isn't worth it to feel like this."

Decisions the children might make:

_____

_____

Family A

Ben, the three-year-old, had been up a lot during the night, so they all went off to visit the doctor. The doctor said Ben had an ear infection and gave them a prescription to have filled by the pharmacist at the drug store. When they got home, Mom said to Ben, "Take this honey. Pills always make you feel better." Last week when Ben's sister was sick and Grandmother gave her medicine, Gram said, "Look honey, the doctor said to take this medicine exactly as the directions say to."

Decisions the children might make:

_____

_____

Family B

Ben, the three-year-old, had been up a lot during the night, so they all went off to visit the doctor. The doctor said Ben had an ear infection and gave them a prescription to have filled by the pharmacist at the drug store. When they got home, Mom said to Ben, "Take this honey. The doctor says it will take the pain out of your ear and help it heal." Grandma said, "Doctors never give you strong enough medicine. I'd take two." Mom put the bottle of pills away.

Decisions the children might make:

_____

_____

Family A

Mother said she needed a cup of coffee and that they should all watch TV and relax for a while. They watched a comedian act drunk. They laughed and laughed. Mom laughed too. Grandmother said she didn't think it was funny to be drunk.

Decisions the children might make:

_____

_____

Family B

Mother wanted to sit down with a cup of coffee. They all gathered at the TV set. They watched a comedian act drunk. Mom laughed. Then she said, "I don't know why I am laughing. This comedian has rubber legs and it's easy to laugh at him, but drunkenness isn't funny in real life. It causes lots of problems." Grandma told Mom she thought Mom was stuffy and that a good laugh at a drunk never hurt anyone.

Decisions the children might make:

_____

_____

Family A

Later in the day everyone helped get ready for the company that was coming for dinner. The kids helped Mom get the beer and drinks ready. Samatha remembered Uncle Will liked having a six-pack of beer in the refrigerator. Mom said Samatha was really thoughtful for remembering Uncle Will liked chilled beer.

Decisions the children might make:

_____

_____

Family B

Later in the day everyone helped get ready for the company that was coming for dinner. The kids helped Mom set the table. Samatha asked if she should put out wine glasses. Mom said yes, they would offer wine and cranberry juice. Samatha remembered that Uncle Will liked having a six-pack of beer in the refrigerator. Mom said, "Samatha, I like the way you are learning to think about what other people want. There are a couple of cans of beer you can put in the refrigerator. I wonder if Uncle Will drinks every day or if coming here is a special occasion."

Decisions the children might make:

_____

_____

Family A

Dad got home later than he had promised. He'd met a client for a beer, and as they were leaving the bar, a friend came in, so they had another beer with him. Mother said she understood and there was just time for a drink before the company was due. Dad made the kids "kiddy cocktails."

Decisions the children might make:

_____

_____

Family B

Dad was sad when he got home. He'd met a client for a beer, and as they were leaving the bar, a friend came in and wanted to have a beer with them. The friend was on his third by the time Dad left. Mother asked if Dad thought that friend had a drinking problem, and Dad said he was afraid so. They both looked concerned. Dad said they needed to get some information about how to help a friend.

Decisions the children might make:

_____

_____

Read each paragraph again, and ask your child to tell you what he or she would think if that happened at your house tomorrow.

Key 6: Talk About Drugs

Children want their parents to initiate talking knowledgeably about alcohol and other drugs and their effects.

The Student Drug Question Survey, 1991

Three hundred young people (fourth through twelfth grades) in five U.S. cities and states responded to questions prepared by the authors of this book. Two school communities surveyed were in the inner city and had a diverse student population.

Of the young people surveyed

- 72 percent wanted their parents to know the facts about drugs and to share that information with their children.

- 65 percent wanted their parents to tell their children *not to use drugs.*

- 40 percent wanted their parents to help and support their children if they were involved with drugs.

One other response that we believe is significant is that 12 percent wanted their parents to stop using drugs or involving their children in drug use.

The following is a sample response from the survey. It is from a sixth grade child in an inner-city Minneapolis public school. This response reflects the concern and insight young people have about drug issues.

Drug Questions

List your best 3 questions you would like to know about drugs.

1. How addicting are they?

2. Why do some parents involve their kids in their dealings and allow their kids to do them?

3. Do they really help you to be happy and clear your anger or depression?

What do you want your parents to know about drugs?

Everything that I know.

What do you want your parents to say to you about drugs?

That they are addicting and it's not OK to do them. And that they don't want us doing them.

Parents need to be able to talk with their children about drugs in lots of ways. Here is a starter list.

Facts about alcohol. Whether children live with drinking or with abstinence, they will be exposed to people who drink. Children deserve to know the facts. Use the true/false quiz, page 49, to find out what areas you still need to cover in teaching your children about alcohol.

Choices about alcohol. Talk with your children about each of the following five aspects of drug use.

- The use of alcohol is a personal choice. No one should be pressured to drink or not to drink.

- Alcohol use is not essential for enjoying family or social events. (See Celebrations, page 51.)

- Drinking that leads to impairment or intoxication is unhealthy and risky.

- Drunkenness is not a condition to be admired, laughed at, or taken lightly.

- People who choose to drink need to know when to abstain from drinking.

This list is adapted from the pamphlet
Choices and Influences,
by Roger Svendsen and Tom Griffin.

Abstinence. Ask your child to take the true/false quiz on page 49, When to Abstain from Using Alcohol or Other Drugs. Discuss the reasons for abstinence.

Drugs—your body—what drugs do. Ask your child to take the true/false quiz Facts About Alcohol, page 49. When you want information about specific drugs, turn to page 123; about the effects of drugs or about stages of drug use, to page 115.

Concerns about friends. Parents' ways of handling drug use by children's friends are based on family values. See the Suggestion Circles, pages 47 and 48.

Your position on your child's using alcohol or drugs. Be sure your children know exactly where you stand. Don't assume they know if you haven't talked clearly and honestly with them. (See Values, page 30.)

Suggestion Circle

My teenage son is concerned about his friend's drug use. What can I say?

Think about these ideas and decide what you would do.

- Talk it over with your son and ask him what he wants to do about it.

- Ask your son if he wants you to call this friend's parent to discuss what your son has shared.

- If your son wants you to, talk to the friend about *your* concerns about his drug use.

- Give your son information about drug abuse to share with his friend.

- Tell your son he is not allowed to be with this friend anymore.

- Spend time talking about drugs, use, abuse, and so on, with your son. Make clear what is OK and what is not OK in your family.

- Tell your son how much you appreciate his sharing the information, and let him know you will help him deal with his friend.

- Ask the school counselor for advice.

- Does this friend drive? If so, ask your son not to ride with him. Help your son make other arrangements.

Thanks to Project Charlie, Jacksonville, FL

Suggestion Circle

My eight-year-old son has a nice friend, but the friend's brother uses drugs. What do I say when my son wants to play at their house?

Think about these ideas and decide what you would do.

- Say no. Allow them to play only at your house.

- Say, "I'm glad you told me about it. Your friend is great. I can't let you go somewhere unsafe. You can play here."

- Ask your child what he thinks about it, and find out what his beliefs are about drugs.

- Explain more about the harmful effects of drugs.

- After each visit, ask your son if the brother has gotten help for his problem. Express caring.

- Ask the friend what he thinks about drugs.

- Let him play there if the house is close by and you are sure your son knows when the brother is high or drunk and will come directly home if he suspects that.

- Explain that the friend doesn't have to use drugs just because someone close to him does.

Thanks to Mai Vang, Eagan, MN

Activity—When to Abstain from Using Alcohol or Other Drugs

True/False Quiz

____ When recovering from chemical dependency.

____ When under legal drinking age.

____ When pregnant or nursing.

____ When operating equipment—cars, motorcycles, power tools, firearms, boats, etc.

____ When swimming, skiing, climbing, or doing other risky physical activities.

____ When working or studying.

____ When performing in athletics or fine arts.

____ When taking certain medications.

____ When it is against your religious belief or personal value decisions.

All of the above are important times to abstain. All are true.

Add ten more situations in which your family abstains. For example: before making an important decision.

Activity—Facts About Alcohol

True/False Quiz

____ 1/2 oz. of liquor, a 9 oz. wine cooler, and a 12 oz. bottle of beer contain approximately the same amount of alcohol.

_____ Eating while drinking slows down the absorption of alcohol into the bloodstream.

_____ As adults age, their metabolisms change, reducing the amount of alcohol they can safely consume.

_____ Fatigue and emotions such as frustration, anger, and loneliness sometimes increase the effects of alcohol on a person's behavior.

_____ Because of differences in body composition and chemistry, females will be affected more than males of equal weight after drinking the same amount of alcohol.

_____ Different ethnic groups respond to alcohol in different ways, both biologically and socially.

_____ Alcohol can retard the emotional and social growth of a young person.

_____ Drinking under age is illegal. However, exceptions do occur when alcohol is being used religiously and ceremonially, as with communion or the family Passover dinner.

_____ Despite all precautions, alcohol-related problems can occur, and it is estimated that about one-fourth of all American families are directly impaired by the effects of alcohol.

Answers: all true.

Adapted from Svendsen and Griffin

Key 7: Value Drug-Free Celebrations

Learning ways to celebrate, play, and have fun without the aid of alcohol or other drugs is an important deterrent to drug abuse because it models healthy choices.

Suggestion Circle

Students report that one of the reasons they use drugs is to have fun (See Search).

How can we celebrate without having alcohol be part of the celebration?

Think about these ideas and decide what you would do.

- Replace alcoholic drinks with nonalcoholic drinks that are pretty and served in the same pretty glasses.

- If you are invited as a family to a celebration where alcohol will be served, talk about it in advance and decide what to do.

- Choose a new group to celebrate with if your current group can't have fun without alcohol.

- Let each family member take turns planning a drug-free celebration for a holiday, a birthday, an anniversary, a family member's achievement, or a celebration of just being together. Create your own traditions. (See Plan for Action, page 71)

- Ask for the kids' input. Be willing to do a celebration that they have planned.

- How wonderful to celebrate and remember it clearly in the future.

Thanks to AA Group, St. Paul, MN

Key 8: Cherish Rituals and Traditions

As parents we need to realize that traditions and rituals are part of the consistent structure that gives stability to children's lives. It is our job to create rituals and traditions that are meaningful for every family member.

Children who grow up in alcoholic family systems are less likely to abuse drugs if these families have maintained family rituals in spite of the alcoholism (Wolin et al., pp. 201, 202).

Family rituals offer support, stability, meaning, and a chance to participate. Examples:

- Eating dinner as a family and discussing value issues
- Preparing special foods for certain holidays
- Fishing on the opening day of the season
- Calling relatives on certain days
- Going certain places together regularly
- A parent bringing gifts home from a trip

Family rituals grow out of family values. Offering a wedding toast with champagne or sparkling juice reflects one value, getting drunk at weddings, another value. If you have rituals that do not reflect your values, you can change them. Ask your children what your family rituals are. "What do we always do at birthdays?" (for example). You may be surprised. Rituals speak to a deep inner part of us, and it is important for children to be involved in them, to help create them, and to help evaluate them.

Especially important are rituals that celebrate life transitions: birth, graduations, weddings, deaths, and so on. Unfortunately some young people consider getting drunk or high and losing their virginity an "initiation rite."

Suggestion Circle

What are some ideas for a ritual to honor a child's entering puberty?

Think about these ideas and decide what you will do.

- Put the "You are important" plate on the table at the child's place. Congratulate the child on entering a new part of life.

- When my daughter got her first period, her father brought her a lovely chain and pendant.

- Some fathers take their sons on a special hunting trip at about age thirteen.

- Many Jewish families honor it by celebrating their children's Jewishness as young men and women through the Bat or Bar Mitzvah, a religious ritual.

- For girls, at first menstruation, do a women's honoring circle with a group of women each giving the girl a gift and a piece of wisdom about becoming a woman.

- For boys, do a men's honoring circle in the same way on the thirteenth birthday.

Thanks to Ramona Oswald, Minneapolis, MN

Activity—Creating a Ritual

Choose an event for which you want to create a special ritual. The following elements of a ritual may all be present, or you may use only three or four. They are not presented in any special order of importance. Select the elements you want to use, design your ritual, and do it. Afterward, as a family, decide if you want to repeat it or change it.

Time. Rituals mark our age, the changes in seasons, and our life transitions.

Place. Location may be very important in some rituals. "Thanksgiving doesn't seem real at a restaurant!"

Oral Element. Most rituals involve a special food or beverage: birthday cake, Easter eggs. Some include a special kiss.

Scent. Orange blossoms, incense, pine boughs.

Light. Bonfires, jack-o'-lanterns, the menorah, the Olympic torch.

Music. Marches, taps, hymns, "our song."

Words. Poetry, litany, chant, pledge, wishes, congratulations.

Movement or Stillness. Bow, stand, salute, march, accept this candle.

Dress. Black tie, costume parties, dress uniforms.

Symbols. Ring, crown, scepter, gavel, cross, Star of David, flag.

Mutual Exchange. "I pledge to you, you pledge to me."

People and Roles. Some roles are assigned, others can be exchanged. "Only the bride can be the bride, but any aunt can pour."

Structure and Flow. Rituals have three parts: an opening, a middle, and a closing.

Key 9: Promote Spiritual Growth

Children need guidance in their spiritual growth.

Young people who say that religion is important to them, attend religious services regularly, and participate in religious youth groups are less likely to use chemicals than those who do not attend (Search). Spirituality is not always equated with formal religion (Stinnett/DeFrain).

Suggestion Circle

What are some ways that I can encourage my child's spiritual growth?

Think about these ideas and decide what you will do.

- Put a spiritual aspect into rituals celebrating milestones like puberty and adulthood, birth, birthdays, weddings, graduations.

- Use the miracle of the seeds and growth to teach awe.

- Set aside individual and family time for prayer.

- As a family, contribute to food shelves and do something to reduce world hunger.

- Encourage your teenager to attend church or synagogue at least three times a month. Let her choose which services or activities to attend.

- Continually emphasize that we are part of something much larger than ourselves.

- As a family, volunteer at a shelter for the homeless.

Thanks to Russell Osnes, Prior Lake, MN

Key 10: Teach Empathy

*Not only do children need to be helped to understand
that caring about others is important, but they need to
learn by helping their parents care for others.*

If children who formerly valued caring about and for others acquire self-serving, hedonistic values, drug abuse is more likely. One of the distressing findings of the Search study is that helping others was valued less by twelfth graders than by sixth graders. Some respondents, mainly boys, assumed more self-serving, hedonistic attitudes as they grew older.

Suggestion Circle

What ways have you found to encourage children to care about others, to be helpful and empathic?

Think about these ideas and decide what you will do.

- Through caring for animals.
- When the kids talk bad about a kid at school or you see it on TV, ask, "How would you feel if you were that person?"
- Teach your children to help you and to be respectful to you as an adult.
- Say, "Don't criticize your neighbors until you have walked a mile in their shoes."

- Do something about world hunger, the poor, or the homeless.
- Get Mary Beth Quiney's book *Why Does That Man Have Such a Big Nose?*
- As a family, volunteer regularly to help others.

Thanks to Marion London, Edina, MN

Key 11: Resolve Grief

*Children need the family to be a safe place
for them to mourn the many losses
they encounter while growing up.*

One of the most valuable lessons children can learn in their families is that they can survive and grow from grief and loss (Search, Stinnett/DeFrain). We parents sometimes try to protect children from loss and distress because we don't want them to experience hurt and pain.

When we gloss over or cover up a loss, we create two additional losses for a child. First, the child loses the chance to learn more about how to grieve and how to grow from the process. Second, the child may not be able to finish grieving that loss and may carry remnants of sadness and loss (even into adult life), which he or she may attempt to relieve with drugs.

We can show children that sadness is a normal, healthy response to loss. We can teach them that it is OK to acknowledge and express hurt and other feelings. We cannot do the grieving for our children, because we cannot measure someone's grief or loss. But our children will know grief. Some of them will have to grieve the loss of relationships and friendships due to drug abuse.

Many people who grew up with alcoholic parents had small and large losses that were denied. Their feelings of grief were minimized or ridiculed. Many of these children learned to hide their feelings so well that as adults they are not conscious of sadness and pain they still carry from the years when they were growing up.

Suggestion Circle

Life is filled with losses as well as gains. Some things lost can never be regained. How do we help children grieve losses and teach them that saying good-bye is a regular part of life?

Think about these ideas and decide what you will do.

- Share any information about a loss that the child asks for—don't hide it or sugarcoat it.

- Allow children to see you sad or angry or crying when you experience a loss, and not only for a death.

- Help them create a ritual around loss or death (for example, a gift for a friend who is moving or a funeral for a dead pet).

- Help children verbalize their feelings, what they liked, what they miss, and what they didn't like.

- Do take kids to the wakes and funerals when you go.

- If a child loses something, don't immediately go out and buy something new to replace it.

- Acknowledge their pain for a final loss and explain that it is not the end of the world even if it feels that way. Use the Affirmations, pages 23–27.

- Get Gesme's *Help! for Kids About Moving* workbook.

- Tell your child your religious beliefs about loss and death.

- Show pictures of great-grandparents—to be gone is not to be forgotten.

Thanks to Deane Gradous, Wayzata, MN

Suggestion Circle

How do I help my daughter with her grief? She just found out her good friend is on drugs. She is upset and feels betrayed.

Think about these ideas and decide what you will do.

- Listen. Hold her in a tender, nurturing way.

- Help her think through whether they can still be friends.

- Let her discuss her attitude toward drug use.

- Don't condemn. Ask her what she wants to do.

- For a while if she gets angry at you, don't take it personally. It may be anger from grieving.

- Tell her about the steps in grieving so she won't be surprised.

- Acknowledge her feelings of betrayal—be there for her—and ask what she needs from you.

- Get to know more about her friend and how to get help for her friend.

- Suggest she talk with the school counselor.

- Encourage her *not* to maintain a friendship with someone who is on drugs. That is false loyalty.

- Acknowledge her pain, but emphasize that her friend is not doing it to hurt her, but because she has a problem or a loss.

Thanks to Patty Gardner, Eden Prairie, MN

Activity—Identify Family Rules About Grieving

Each family member thinks of two situations when someone in your family experienced loss. Examples: a friend moved, loss of a job.

Share what the loss was, and what the family did and said. Examples:

When Grandpa died, Daddy never cried, and he was complimented for "not breaking down."

When kitty died, you were sad too, and you helped me have a funeral.

When puppy died, you told me not to be sad and got me a new one.

When my brother got a ticket for drunk driving, you told us not to tell anyone.

Then list the rules about grieving and loss that your family offered or that you assumed. Examples:

Men don't cry when someone dies. Showing grief is "breaking down" or a sign of weakness.

If you lose something or someone, your family helps you grieve.

When you lose something, ignore your feelings and replace it.

Don't tell anyone or talk about your grief.

Together look at the rules to see if they support each aspect of grieving: shock and denial, anger, sadness and depression, fear, coping skills, bargaining, acceptance, empathy, and integration. To learn more about the steps, read Kubler-Ross's *On Death and Dying*.

Change any rules you need to.

Ask each person to choose one or more affirmations (pages 23–27) to support each new rule about grieving.

Key 12: Practice Delayed Gratification

*The degree of freedom children will experience
as adults may depend partly on how they
learn to defer the urge to "have it all" now.*

Now! Now! Me! Me!

If you can't wait, you take drugs.
Drugs are instead of problem solving.
Drugs are instead of feeling OK about oneself.
Drugs are instead of meaningful relationships.
Drugs are instead of feeling your feelings.
Drugs are about me, me, now, now!

Learning how to delay gratification, to wait, not to have it all now, and to have that be all right gives a child a bulwark against drug abuse.

Wait and Enough

Children learn the skills of when and how to delay gratifications

- By being taught the difference between needs and wants: needs are gratified quickly if possible; wants can wait

- By learning the concepts of "enough" and "enough for now"

- By watching older members of the family delay wants and talk about that as an important, OK part of life

- By having small gratifications delayed when they are young and by being rewarded
- By having large gratifications delayed when they are older and by being rewarded

Activity—I Want It Now

Each of the following examples of delayed gratification has two parental responses. Check the one that encourages the child's ability to wait.

1. The infant cries in his crib while Mom finishes dressing.

____ Mom picks the baby up and coos, "Poor little one! She had to wait. Mommy's sorry."

____ Mom calls, "I'm coming—thanks for calling me." She picks up baby and says in a cheerful tone, "Good job waiting! I'm here now."

2. The toddler is fussing for his juice.

____ Dad says in a singsong voice, "Watch me go to the refrigerator; next I go to the cupboard. I'm fixing Rudy's juice. Here it is."

____ Dad says in a solicitous voice, "Oh, Rudy, I know it's hard for you to wait. I'll hurry!"

3. The preschooler is demanding to go outside to play.

____ Mom stops whatever she is doing, finds the child's jacket, puts it on him and takes him out.

____ In a pleasant voice Mom says, "That will be great. I'll help you with your jacket after we pick up your blocks. Where is the block basket?"

4. The grade school child is whining as she waits for a ride to the store.

____ Dad says, "If you are in a hurry to go, help me finish this chore. If you aren't in a hurry, just stop whining. Which will it be?"

____ Dad says, "I have so much to do, it seems as if I never have time to take you someplace when you want to go. Won't it be great when you can drive?"

5. The teenager is lobbying for a new set of drums.

____ Mom says, "I don't have the money right now, but you want them so much I'll take out a loan. They can be your Christmas present."

____ Mom says, "I'm waiting to hear your plan. How much do they cost? What can you contribute? How long will that take? Then we'll decide. You are good at that kind of planning."

Key: Delayed gratification responses: 1—b; 2—a; 3—b; 4—a; 5—b

Make up your own examples and think how you would respond if you were teaching instant gratification and how you would respond if you were teaching delayed gratification. Of course, not every request needs to be delayed. Watch your child. If your child seems to be passive, help the child ask and then respond quickly. If your child is in a "now, now, me, me" stage, ease in a few more delays if he or she is two or under. Arrange many more if he or she is three or older.

If you are in a "now, now, me, me" stage, make up some adult examples and identify the instant and delayed gratification messages or instant gratification justifications you could give yourself.

Be aware that TV and other media encourage viewers to believe that they deserve instant gratification (see Media, page 94.)

We live in a culture that wants things to be quick, high quality, and cheap. In manufacturing this might be possible. In human development that attitude becomes a thief.

Activity—The Enough Continuum

Overindulged children often have difficulty identifying what is enough.

Place five signs on the floor in order.

Not Enough	Just Enough	Enough	Abundance	Too Much

On 3 × 5 cards write things that children want enough of. Ask the children to contribute ideas.

Examples: toys, donuts, shirts, outings, shoelaces, games, books, rides, lessons, sports equipment, attention, clean laundry, space in the house, music.

In turn, each child chooses a card. He or she stands on each sign and tells what would be not enough, just enough, enough, abundance, or too much of the item on the card. Then he or she asks for affirmations and challenges. The family affirms the child for creative, thoughtful, or humorous ways of describing a point. If there is a point on which they disagree with him or her, they can ask three challenge questions. Tell which sign you are challenging. (1) Why did you choose that example? (2) Did you think about what would happen to other people if you had that? (3) What would happen to you if you had that?

Play the game many times. Change the example cards as children mature. If your children are old enough, use the dictionary and discuss the meaning of such words as *adequate, sufficient, satisfying a need, scarcity,* and *overindulgence.*

Key 13: Share History of Drug Use, Abuse, or Addiction in the Family

Children deserve to know that they are more likely to develop drug/alcohol problems if there is a history of these problems among family members.

There are no clear-cut answers to why people become alcoholic. However, alcoholism is up to four times as prevalent in people from families with a history of alcohol or other drug abuse (MIPH, Jerry Jaker). The cause may be genetic or environmental or both (NIAAA, Farris/Jones)

Suggestion Circle

The alcoholism in my family is considered shameful and is kept secret. How can I tell my kids about the alcoholism without having the whole family mad at me?

Think about these ideas and decide what you will do.

- I told and they denied it, but now my child knows.

- Read Claudia Black's *It Will Never Happen to Me* for ideas about how to tell.

- I told my kids, and my sister is still mad at me.

- I told my kids, and when they asked about it, my family went up the wall. We ended up getting help, and now we are talking to one another about lots of things we didn't talk about before.

- Shame is powerful stuff. You will have to risk their being mad.

- Risk it. Maybe some other family members will be glad to have it out in the open.

Thanks to Carole Gesme, Minnetonka, MN

Suggestion Circle

I don't know the history of drug use or abuse in my family. How do I go about finding out, and what do I look for?

Think about these ideas and decide what you will do.

- You or someone talk to your parents about family history, and have them ask about drugs as part of that.

- Ask your mother about her parents and grandparents, how they lived and how they died. Also ask your father.

- Watch in your family of origin for signs of addictive behaviors such as smoking, food bingeing, workaholism.

- Ask other relatives to tell you stories about your family. The drug information will come out in the stories of other behaviors. For example, in my family a feud between family members turned out to be about alcoholism.

- If you are adopted, contact your social worker or agency to see if they have information in your file. Assume alcoholism may be in your background.

- You can record an interview with the oldest family member. Ask all sorts of questions about the family history.

- Ask and listen carefully to family stories, noting both what is and isn't said. If there are consistent secrets, you may have cause to wonder.

- Ask people in the family how they define alcoholism. You may need to use other words such as "heavy drinkers."

- Read Wegscheider-Cruse's *Choice Making* to learn about family roles in alcoholic systems. See if any of that information fits your family.

Thanks to Pat Miller, Wayzata, MN

Suggestion Circle

We have never discussed our family's history of alcohol/drug abuse with our children. How do we start?

Think about these ideas and decide what you will do.

- Just do it.

- Say, "I want you to have this information," not "Do you want this information?"

- One way is to talk about it after the children have seen someone drunk or on drugs on the street. Talk about what that means, and who in your family uses drugs and why and how they do.

- Look at old photo albums. Tell the story of family members.

- Keep your own emotional issues separate from the factual information about a person's chemical dependency. Don't get into name calling. The person has a problem or a disease.

- When you find newspaper or magazine stories about alcohol or other drugs, use them as a starting point to ask what the kids already know and then ask, "Did you know that . . . " in a matter-of-fact way.

- Use a drug-related video such as *Clean and Sober* or the *Suzanne Sommers Story* to start talking.

- As a family, fill out a family tree and document drug use.

- Don't worry about doing it right, just begin.

Thanks to Pamela L. Searles, Minnetonka, MN

Key 14: Make Decisions, Plan for Action

*It is important for children to know how to make
decisions and solve problems before
they are confronted with pressures to use drugs.*

Decisions Are Based on Values

Children have learned values, piece by piece, day by day, in their families from the day they were born. The specific decisions a child makes about using drugs—when, where, how much, with whom—will be based on all those earlier decisions about values and how to behave. Parents help children clarify and claim their values by activities such as the ones suggested in Values, page 30.

Parents can emphasize that because the decisions children make about drugs can shape their lives, it is important for children to learn decision-making skills before the occasion to use drugs arises.

Parents can neglect their children by making all of the decisions for them. When parents make too many of the decisions, children are deprived of the chance to practice their decision-making skills.

When parents teach decision-making techniques, they strengthen their children's ability to resist drugs. The family can involve children in family decisions whenever that is appropriate. Look at what some parents let kids make decisions about at every age (see below). Practice the group and individual decision-making activities on pages 73–75.

Suggestion Circle

What are some safe things to let children make decisions about?

Think about these ideas and decide what you will do.

Preschool Age

- Which shirt to wear to school
- Whether to take a bath before or after dinner
- What book to read
- Which toys to play with

Grade School Age

- Who their friends are
- Choosing household tasks from parent's list of options
- Taking turns choosing family activities
- Which school pictures to choose
- What extracurricular activity they want to try

Teenage

- What outside activities to become involved in
- Clothing
- Choosing who to date and who not to date
- Choosing possible vocations and careers
- Planning how to spend time with the family

Thanks to Sandra Sittko, Eagan, MN

Activity—Group Decision Making

It is important not to make the decisions for your children that they can make for themselves. Prepare your child for personal decision making by using family decision making at least once a week. Whenever possible, let children help make the final choice, but help them see the options and possible long-term results.

Use the following format next time a family problem comes up, or make up problems to practice.

State the problem: Whether to watch TV

Example:

Alternative Solutions	Consequences	
	Short Term	**Long Term**
1. Father decides	Everyone watches sports	Kids don't learn to make decisions
2. Mother decides	She decides no TV	Kids don't learn to make decisions
3. Family votes	Some are pleased, some aren't	Parents lose control of what programs kids watch
4. Parents select suitable programs; children choose from those	Some are pleased, some aren't	Parents monitor program's suitability and kids learn to make choices

Each family member ranks the alternative solutions:

Mom   Dad   Child   Child   Child

Family compares the separate lists.
Family discusses, negotiates, and decides.
Celebrate improving your ability to make decisions.

Activity—Individual Planning and Decision Making

Children learn decision-making skills by practicing those skills in planning sessions.

Identify any problem, possibly one concerning drugs, that your child might face. Examples: Someone on the playground offers my child pills. My teenager is having a party and friends arrive with liquor. My child rides to a party with a friend and the friend is high when it is time to go home.

Write each of the following steps of the planning/decision-making process on a separate card.

> State the problem.
>
> Identify your goal.
>
> Consider your options.
>
> Consider the consequences of each option.
>
> Consider your values.
>
> Consider your feelings.
>
> Ask for help.
>
> Gather more information.
>
> Decide.
>
> Act.
>
> Evaluate your decision.

Put aside the Decide, Act, and Evaluate cards to use later.

Help your child consider each of the eight cards in the order she chooses. A card may be used more than once.

Pick up the Decide, Act, and Evaluate cards and ask:

> What is your decision?
>
> What will your action be?
>
> How can we evaluate this plan?

Affirm the child for doing this planning and point out specific examples of clear thinking.

Ask if she would like some more ideas on what decision she could make or what action to take. If so, run a Suggestion Circle for her. You or she could do a phone circle (see page 149).

Key 15: Respect Feelings

*It is our job as parents to teach and model
for children how to accept, understand, label,
and appropriately express feelings.*

Feelings are an important source of information for children. Parents need to encourage their children to talk about feelings from an early age. Parents need not feel the same way a child does in order to show a child that he or she is loved unconditionally, is important, and is accepted. Parents need to accept all of a child's feelings. Feelings tell children about their responses to their world.

Alcoholism is a "feelings" disease. People who are alcoholic or chemically dependent often have trouble accepting or expressing their feelings. When they want relief from emotional pain, they know that alcohol or other drugs will work to deaden the pain. Drugs are dependable. Family and friends are not always dependable. People come to depend on drugs to take the hurt away. Temporarily this works, but it doesn't work well. Instead of finding the elusive relief, people often become addicted, causing problems with family members, friends, work, and school. This is one reason it is so important to learn healthy ways to handle feelings.

Suggestion Circle

Sometimes I feel so angry I have a hard time keeping my cool when I communicate with my family. What can I do to reduce my anger before I talk with them?

Think about these ideas and decide what you will do.

- Count to ten and take a few deep breaths.
- Walk, run, or exercise for twenty minutes.
- Relax and listen to music.
- Think about a time when you were having fun with the family member you are angry with now, or think about positive traits this person has.
- Write about how you are feeling.
- Draw a picture of your anger.
- Rip up old newspapers or magazines and throw them about. Then pick them up.
- Take a shower to wash away the negative feelings.
- Figure out what you are so angry about, and do something to solve the problem.
- Read the *Help! for Parents* books by Clarke et al. and use the Fuss Box activity described there.
- Think about what other feelings you might have in this same situation.

Thanks to Joan Baraf, North Hills, NY

Suggestion Circle

Sometimes my teenagers get into despair about the ozone layer or the nuclear threat or the environment or whatever. How can I help them?

Think about these ideas and decide what you will do.

- Keep children of all ages involved in community activities that will lessen one of these threats.

- Tell them how you have lived through some of your despair.

- Keep your communication open so they talk with you about their despair.

- Find a group of people who are working on making your teenager's area of concern better.

- Have them think of three things they can do about the thing they are in despair about to show them they can make a difference.

- As a family, study the problem and do something about it.

- Subscribe to an environmental magazine for information and ways to get involved.

- Listen. Don't make critical judgments about their concerns.

- Tell them what you are doing to help.

Thanks to Maggie Lawrence, Edmonds, WA

Activity—What I Can Do with My Feelings

Ask each family member to pick one feeling face (see page 80) and tell about a time he or she felt each way and what he or she did. Then read the "I can . . . " section and ask that person to think of two other things he or she could do next time.

When I feel *sad*, I can tell someone I feel sad. I can cry. I can ask for comfort and help. I can get support.

When I feel *happy*, I can tell someone I feel happy. I can celebrate by myself or with others.

When I feel *angry*, I can tell someone I feel angry. I can ask for help to solve problems. I can ask questions, gather information, and get help.

When I feel *scared*, I can tell someone I feel scared. I can find safety and comfort. I can ask for information.

When I feel *ashamed or embarrassed*, I can tell someone how I feel and what is bothering me. I can apologize. I can ask for help. I can know I'm OK—it is my behavior that may need to change.

When I feel *mixed up*, I can tell someone I feel mixed up. I can use the Feeling Faces Board on page 80 to show all of the ways I am feeling. I can ask for help.

Use the affirmations on pages 23–27 to help you accept your children's feelings.

needed • jealous • glad • hurt • lucky • tired • joyful • surprised

unwanted • trusted • alone • happy • dirty • worried • frightened

special • stupid • brave • helpless • smart • guilty • depressed • confident • rejected • free • disgusted

carefree • embarrassed • scared • lovable • ashamed • capable • sad • excited • angry • alive • let down

© 1985 Carole Gesme

Key 16: Resist Negative Peer Pressure

Resisting peer pressure is a skill that allows children to make their own decisions about their behavior. The parents' job is to teach children this skill.

To be part of a group, to be accepted, is very important for all of us. At some time, in order to be part of a group, most of us have allowed someone to pressure us into doing something we had not intended to do. This is called negative peer pressure. Children deserve to be taught how to resist it (USDHHS, MSSR).

Peer pressure may be given

- verbally—from blatant threats to subtle innuendo
- by body language—words do not have to be spoken
- internally—the voice inside telling us how to conform.

  Methods of peer pressure include

- Reasoning: "Everyone else is doing it. Just one won't hurt."
- Criticism: "When did you become such a goody-goody? You spoil our fun."
- Rejection: "We won't ask you any more. We only like people who are like us."
- Snubbing: leaving, walking away, ignoring.

Children who have practiced resisting peer pressure before the situation occurs are better able to resist all types of pressure. Go through the Suggestion Circle ideas on things kids can do to resist peer pressure. Then practice the role play Resisting Negative Peer Pressure several times.

Suggestion Circle

How can I teach my child not to ride with people under the influence?

Think about these ideas and decide what you will do.

- Say, "If for some reason you cannot reach me, call a cab."
- Insist that he keep bus fare and phone numbers with him.
- Respect your child when she refuses to go to a party.
- Participate in MADD and SADD activities (see page 148).
- Teach children ways to recognize if a teenager or adult friend has been drinking or is high. Support them for asking for adult support or intervention when they need it.
- Don't let preoccupation with your own problems cause you not to notice that your children are in unsafe places.
- Have a code word your children can use if friends or baby-sitting employers are listening to their phone call for help.
- Emphasize that life is more important than a ride. Tell your child it is really cool to stay alive.
- If an adult driver has been drinking, say, "I promised to call home before I left." Use your code word for help.

Thanks to Kay Joppru, Minnetonka, MN

Suggestion Circle

What are some things kids can do to resist negative peer pressure?

Think about these ideas and decide what you will do.

- Say "No." Practice saying no several times a day in front of a mirror.

- Say "No" over and over, like a broken record. "No, no thanks, nope, no way, take a hike."

- Say, "No, I don't want to." "I'm not interested." "I don't like the idea." "I'm in training."

- Change the subject. Say, "No thanks, where did you get that new sweater?"

- Name the consequences or give information. "Why would you want to use drugs? They are boring." "These drugs are illegal. We could get into trouble."

- Suggest another activity. "Let's go roller blading."

- Find an excuse. "I can't drink because I'd get kicked off the team." "My parents won't let me." "I have to go to work."

- Ignore the person.

- Leave the situation. Walk away.

- Find other kids to hang around with.

Thanks to Jim Epperly, Minneapolis, MN

Activity—Practice Resisting Negative Peer Pressure

The family can practice resisting negative pressure. Have each family member choose examples from the list below or make up one of his or her own. Other family members role play putting on the pressure. Practice again and again, applying more pressure and in different ways.

After each role play, identify which methods of resisting peer pressure were used. Invent more of your own.

Examples:

- It is Saturday afternoon, and your family is on its way out the door to spend the day relaxing at the beach. A friend calls with a ticket for a baseball game you want to attend.

- You failed your last two tests and feel terrible. A girl offers you a red pill and promises it will make you feel better.

- You are at your cousin's wedding. All of the young people are drinking. Your parents are not around to see what you are doing.

- Your parents are out of town. You have a few friends over, and they start to look for some alcohol.

- You promised the family you'd be home at 6:00 for dinner and your friend begs you to stop for a drink.

- Using the affirmations for structure (page 27), have each family member choose the messages that would help him or her resist peer pressure in each of the above examples. Read the affirmations for structure, or copy the ovals and give a set to each child.

Key 17: Support Positive Peer Pressure

*Children need to learn how to make
and maintain healthy friendships.*

Learning to choose, make, and keep friends with healthy positive values is as important in drug abuse prevention as learning to resist peer pressure. Also, persons recovering from drug abuse will need support in finding new friends. (MIPH, USDHHS, MSSR)

Suggestion Circle

How can I help my child make and keep friends?

Think about these ideas and decide what you will do.

- Ask her to describe what a friend is.
- Go to the library and get books about friendship, for example, *Growing Up Feeling Good* by Ellen Rosenberg.
- Make a list of five people she would like to be friends with.
- Say, "Choose somebody you want to be friends with. Ask her to play with you. Go for a walk with her."
- Tell your child the kinds of things you do to maintain your friendships.
- Teach her about kindness, politeness, and sharing.
- Tell her why you think she would be a neat friend.

- Make a list of all the places she could find a friend.
- Help her practice ways of starting a conversation.

Thanks to Chris Ternand, M.D., Minnetonka, MN

Suggestion Circle

My fifteen-year-old daughter says, "My best friend has started using drugs. That's not for me. How do I start making new friends? All the kids already have friends."

Think about these ideas and decide what you will do.

- Say, "I'm here for you."
- See if there are natural helpers at school for her to connect with.
- Celebrate her decision to make new friends.
- Allow her to grieve the loss of a good friend.
- If her school has a support group for kids who don't use drugs, she could investigate that.
- She could join a club about one of her interests.
- She can look lots of places for new friends, even new groups of friends—school, church, community clubs, sports activities, work.
- Help her list the qualities she wants in a friend and the qualities she brings to a friendship.
- Remind her that there is no right number of friends. What other friends does she have now?
- Talk about your own friendships and how some of them have changed or ended. Tell how you grieved.

Thanks to students from Roosevelt High, Kent, OH

Activity—How to Use Thoughts, Feelings, and Actions

Children need to learn to think about their feelings and feel about their thinking.

- Help your children define the difference between thoughts, feelings, and actions.

Thoughts: Our thoughts are our opinions, conclusions, what we understand, and what we have experienced.

Feelings: Our emotions can be anger, sadness, happiness, fear, or embarrassment. Other people do not know what we are thinking or feeling.

Actions: What we do and what we say or what other people can see are our actions.

Our thoughts, feelings, and actions all work together, sometimes so fast that we forget they are all separate.

- Teach children that in a given situation, we have a thought that triggers a feeling or a feeling that triggers a thought and produces an action.

Example: John has just returned to school after completing drug treatment. He says, "I won't have any friends, now that I don't smoke dope."

Ask him what he thinks ("No one will like me."), what he feels (rejected and angry), and what his action will be (to isolate himself).

- Given that same situation, ask what different thought would lead to a more positive action.

Example:

Thought: "I'll figure out how to make new friends."

Feeling: Nervous and excited.

Action: Joins the drug-free support group.

Think of other examples to practice with your child.

Key 18: Practice Positive Communication Skills

Children need to practice effective communication skills—both speaking and listening—within the family.

Effective communication is a crucial drug prevention strategy. Adolescent drug users have frequently reported that their families communicated primarily negative messages to one another, if they communicated at all (MSSR).

Suggestion Circle

My children say I don't listen to them. What can I do?

Think about these ideas and decide what you will do.

- Put the paper down and look them in the eyes.
- Schedule a special time to listen to each child.
- Don't interrupt them when they are talking.
- When you are listening, don't tell them what they are saying is wrong all the time.
- Let them know you are listening by repeating what you think they said.
- Don't ridicule or make fun of them for talking.
- Don't follow their information with a lecture.
- Ask them how they will know if you are listening.

• Schedule family meetings. Use a "talking stick," which is held by the person talking while others listen.

Thanks to Bob Elliott, Minneapolis, MN

Activity—Open and Closed Responses

Your responses to your children's concerns can encourage or discourage communication.

Closed response: If you respond to your son with a *closed* response, your child hears that his feelings are not important and possibly wrong. He may even feel he has done something wrong.

Open response: When you offer your son an open or supportive response that asks him how he feels, and express concern and support, he will hear that his feelings are accepted.

For the following situation, identify which responses are *open* and which are *closed*.

Your son, age nine, comes in the door with a sad face. He says, "Everyone was invited to Ben's birthday party but me."

_____ 1. "I never did like Ben's mom. I'm glad you aren't going."

_____ 2. "There will be other birthday parties."

_____ 3. "You look so sad—are you feeling sad? Let's talk more about it."

_____ 4. "It might be hard not being invited—how are you feeling?"

_____ 5. "What did you do to Ben that he decided not to invite you?"

_____ 6. "How are you feeling about that? Tell me more about it."

_____ 7. "I'm busy. Go talk to your father."

_____ 8. "I'm sorry I have to leave right now. We'll tell Dad, and you can talk with him now. I'll talk later if you want to."

Answers: 1, 2, 5, 7 are closed; 3, 4, 6, 8 are open.

Contracts and Promises

Parents can set up "quality time" periods with preschoolers. With school-age children and teenagers, "scheduling" quality time often doesn't work. You have to spend enough time with them for quality time to occur when they are ready to talk. Listening is an important part of quality time. If you cannot listen all the way through at that moment, contract to listen later on.

Promises

Sometimes we make promises instead of contracts.

"Sam, I really want to listen, but I'm running late for work. I promise to talk to you after work at 4:00 P.M."

Even if you are ready to talk with your child at 4:00, that may not be the time when he is ready or available to talk.

Contracts

However, when we *contract,* we build important safeguards into the listening process.

"Sam, I really want to listen to you but I'm running late for work. Could we talk later?"
Sam offers to talk at dinner.
"At dinner is fine with me. We'll order in pizza so I'm not preoccupied with making dinner. See you at 5:30?"
Sam agrees.

You hold your part of the contract. If your child does not show up, confront him and set up a new contract.

When we use contracting to ensure that we will listen to our children, we are also teaching them how to make contracts, a useful tool.

Change Chain

A request to change behaviors or attitudes can be made in many ways. These eleven ways of requesting are presented as an option chain to remind us that since a chain is as strong as its weakest link, when we neglect to consider or use any of

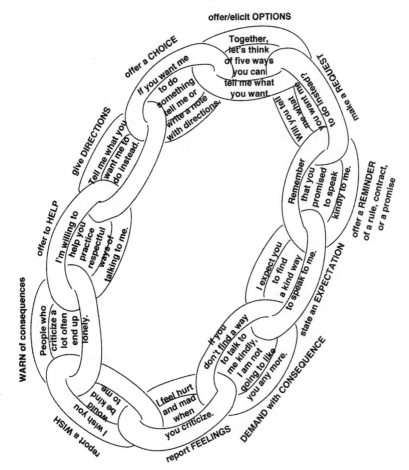

these options, we are limiting our power and our effectiveness. Not all of these will always be effective, so for any given problem identify the eleven different ways a request could be made and then choose the one that is most appropriate to the specific situation.

Example: I want someone to stop criticizing me.

Take an example of your own. Write a response for each of the eleven links. Choose the ones that are most likely to be effective. Try them out.

Activity—Talking

Use positive, self-esteem-building messages to encourage open communication. (See the Affirmations, pages 23–27, and Self-Esteem, page 19.)

We can teach children skills for asking for what they need by the ways we ask for things. Use the Change Chain to assess how your family makes requests.

- Study the links of the chain.

- Identify the three or four ways you prefer to be asked.

- Guess which three or four ways your child likes to be asked.

- Ask your child to identify the ways he or she likes to be asked.

- Ask you child to guess the ways you like to be asked.

- Compare your lists.

- Discuss and practice ways to ask each other considerately.

- Remember that a chain is as strong as its weakest link, so practice identifying eleven ways of making the same request.

- Notice that some links won't be suitable for some requests. For instance, we don't tell a young child we wish he or she wouldn't run in the street.

For Better or For Worse®   **by Lynn Johnston**

Key 19: Resist Media Messages

The media send constant, persuasive messages that drug abuse is OK. Children deserve to know how to recognize and resist those messages.

Parents today are faced with the problem of raising children who are overexposed to television and movies. For most children, time spent watching television far exceeds time spent doing homework and even hours in school (Search).

Television is a persistent source of information about drug use and other health issues. However, much of the information is distorted, especially during commercials. When children watch TV, they often get messages about drug use that conflict with values taught in the family. For example: your parents say alcohol hurts your body; the media show beautiful, healthy-looking people drinking.

These conflicting messages may both seem true when heard separately, yet when heard together they are confusing.

Parents need to

- Point out and talk about conflicting messages (for example, family: drugs harm bodies; media: drinking is glamorous)

- Honor children's feelings (use the Feeling Faces Board, page 80, to help you identify feelings)

- Talk about each of the conflicting messages and reinforce the family values

Suggestion Circle

As a parent, what can I do about the media messages that tell my child he needs to drink or smoke to be "cool"?

Think about these ideas and decide what you will do.

- Share your standards and beliefs about chemicals.

- Teach your children to understand that media advertising is designed to make money for the sponsor, not to help the buyer.

- Catch your child thinking for herself and praise her for it.

- Read and discuss billboards while driving.

- Ask your child what she needs from you to help her resist this constant assault of messages.

- As a family, watch five different kinds of TV offerings. Notice what beverages are served, how many, and what the messages are about drinking, smoking, and taking drugs.

- Turn off the TV. The kid who watches TV for the national average of six hours a day gets six times the pollution of a kid who watches one hour a day.

- Help your child find "cool" people who don't drink or smoke.

- Create your own ads, billboards, and commercials with your child that say smoking and drinking are not "cool."

Thanks to Physical Education Teachers, New Orleans, LA

Suggestion Circle

How can I protect my child from watching too much TV?

Think about these ideas and decide what you will do.

- On Sunday, pick the week's programs from the TV guide.
- Turn it off.
- Sell the TV set. Fill the house with music, books, crafts, hobbies, and games.
- Set a good example. Turn off a program because it laughs at drunkenness or contains sex or violence, and say why.
- Place a value on regular exercise instead of TV.
- Talk and read with the children instead of watching TV.
- No TV sets in kids rooms.
- Go places as a family instead of watching TV.
- Give young children thirty-minute TV tokens or tickets and help them choose their weekly viewing schedules.
- Match the number of TV viewing hours to the number of homework hours. Only watch TV after homework is done.
- Always watch TV with your young children and discuss what they are viewing.
- Don't let young children watch human violence in shows or on the news. It numbs them.

Thanks to Marion London, Golden Valley, MN

Key 20: Learn About Drugs, Needles, AIDS, and Sex

AIDS has added a whole new fatal aspect to drug abuse.

Suggestion Circle

How can I teach my children about the connection between drugs, needles, AIDS, and sex?

Think about these ideas and decide what you will do.

- Protect young children from too much information. Start about age six and give your children only the information that is appropriate to their ages and situations.

- Suggest to your child that she write about AIDS for a school report. Help her find resources.

- Offer information in lots of little pieces.

- Educate yourself first. Call the National AIDS hotline, 1-800-342-AIDS.

- Talk about a friend or a public figure like Magic Johnson who is HIV positive or has AIDS, and discuss how he or she contracted it.

- Remind teens that any used needles, including steroid needles, contain a drop of blood that can carry HIV.

- Explain that with healthy self-esteem you don't need drugs, and with the AIDS connection they can kill you.

- Check with your school and see what information and programs the teachers offer.

- Watch the Magic Johnson special (on video) with them.

- Talk to your doctor or school nurse about current updates and information. Discuss them with your children.

Thanks to Jean Clarke, Plymouth, MN

Key 21: Connect with Community

Children need to understand the importance of their membership in several communities, including family, school, neighborhood, nation, and humanity.

Children need community. If their families do not keep them meaningfully involved and contributing to a community, children will look for a group where they are valued and where they can belong. Perhaps a gang.

Suggestion Circle

We really don't belong to any group that includes our whole family. What can we do?

Think about these ideas and decide what you will do.

- Identify a family interest and join a club or group about that interest—sports, music, art, travel.
- Watch neighborhood papers for community activities.
- Have people over to signal interest in being part of a group.
- Volunteer together.
- Be involved in the YMCA Family Events Program.
- Pick a church or synagogue and attend regularly.
- Organize a family block party, and plan further activities at that time.

- Join a group that celebrates your ethnic background.
- Regularly spend playtime with families you like.

Thanks to Beth Brekke, Minneapolis, MN

Children need to participate in community in a way that helps others of all ages. Young people who only participate in same-age sports and clubs are just as apt to use drugs and alcohol as those who don't (Search).

Suggestion Circle

How do I help my child participate in community activities?

Think about these ideas and decide what you will do.

- Help your children choose activities that match their natural interests—theirs, not yours.
- Check with your child's friends about things they are doing.
- Contact the school to see what is going on there.
- Adopt a grandparent—someone your child can enjoy, learn from, and help.
- Help the child find volunteer opportunities.
- Recognize that every child has something unique to offer, and help your child find a place to give it.
- Research local community groups and activities and show kids what's available.
- Help the child choose an activity to try—six times (then he or she can choose whether to continue).
- Go with the children and participate with them.

Thanks to Susan Clarke, D.C., St. Paul, MN

Key 22: Encourage Adult Support

Grade school–age children and adolescents need at least three adults outside of their families to ask for help. The teenager, to help form an identity and expand values, needs to have frequent, serious conversations with an adult who is not his or her parent.
Search

Suggestion Circle

How do I help my teenager connect with adults outside of our family?

Think about these ideas and decide what you will do.

- In selecting your own friends, choose people who are good role models and who take time for your kids.
- Teaching your teen to be more respectful of elders makes it easier for her to find helpful adults.
- Have a godparent who is the child's special friend.
- Encourage her to do volunteer work at a retirement center or nursing home.
- Encourage your children to be neighborly.
- Have a group of families get together for intergenerational games or other activities.

- Tell the teenager, "It's OK for you to talk with someone else's parents or another adult when you don't want to talk with me. I did that when I was your age."

- Enlist the support of extended family, especially aunts and uncles. Invite them to spend time with your kids.

- Use formal connections such as Big Brothers.

Thanks to Carol Kuechler, Minneapolis, MN

Key 23: Get Involved with School

*Children need to feel connected with school and
to have positive experiences socially and academically.
Parents need to be directly involved in the school.*

Parents have the right to demand the degree of involvement
in school that they need in order to support their children.

Suggestion Circle

**I've heard that parent involvement in school is part
of preventing drug abuse. I'm scared to go to school,
and my kid doesn't want me involved.**

Think about these ideas and decide what you will do.

- It's not your kid's choice, but don't interfere with her activities.
- Find other parents to work with.
- Talk to the school counselor; ask where you can help.
- Start now and stay active.
- Attend the school activities; volunteer to help.
- Join the PTA or whatever group your school has.
- Go to a general open house to get acquainted with people at the school.

- Get support for yourself about your fear of the school.

- Participate anyway—no excuses—that is an issue that you can control.

Thanks to Darlene Montz, Yakima, WA

Suggestion Circle

What are some ways I can reward my children daily when they do their homework?

Think about these ideas and decide what you will do.

- Turn off the TV and read a book while your children do homework. Later tell each other what you learned.

- Take an adult class and do homework with them.

- Let them know that when they do the best they can do, that's all you expect.

- Make a star chart for the young ones.

- Honor their achievements without comparing them to others.

- Help them set up ground rules for study habits.

- Sometimes fix a snack they would like.

- Show interest in what they're actually learning from the homework and discuss it with them.

- Remind them that feeling good about finishing is a reward.

- Have a special game or fun activity to do after homework is done daily or after so many days in a row.

- If the school does not assign homework, ask for it!

Thanks to Mary Paananen, Seattle, WA

Activity—Your Report Card—with Love

Young people who feel that school is important, do well in school, have educational goals beyond high school, and do at least one hour of homework per school day tend to use alcohol and other drugs less than other students. Homework is also a safeguard against the negative influence of television time and negative peer pressure.

In order to motivate their children to achieve in school, some parents offer rewards, bribe, scold, or punish. Other parents structure time for study, support their child's interests, and let him or her learn in his or her own way. They use report card time to affirm achievement and to offer unconditional love. One parent who asks (not lectures) about report cards does it this way:

Start with the highest grade.

"I see you got an A in history. How did you do that?"

"History is easy and I like it. I did extra credit."

"Great. I'm glad history is easy for you and you like it. Good work!" Pause to savor success. "I see you got a B+ in language arts. How did you do that?"

"I turned in all of my papers on time."

"Good work. I'm glad you are learning the importance of getting your assignments in. I read your essay, and I think you are improving the way you write." Pause to savor success. "I see you got a C in math. How did you do that?"

"I like math, but I messed up on a couple of tests because I hadn't studied enough."

"I'm glad you like math. Have you made plans about keeping up on it?"

"Yes, I will."

"Good." Pause to savor success. "I see you got a D in science. How did you do that?"

"Science is hard for me. I study it more than any other subject, and I still don't get it. Some days I want to skip it."

"Congratulations on sticking with it. Do you need some help from me, or do you need a tutor? I'm willing to help you get what you need."

"No, I'll try it for another quarter by myself."

"All right. If you change your mind, let me know. I'll check in with you in a couple of weeks. Thanks for talking with me about your reports. I'm glad you are my kid!" Pause to savor your success as a supportive parent.

If you want to try this, practice in front of the mirror until you can say, "I see you got an A (or an F). How did you do that?" in *exactly* the same supportive tone of voice and with the same accepting, caring expression. Exactly the same. Then hold the child responsible. If the child does not make promised improvements, confront the child immediately and set appropriate consequences. Carry through.

Keep track of your child's grades. A sudden drop in grades may indicate drug use or other problems.

Key 24: Be Informed About Drugs

In order to be a credible and reliable resource for their children, parents need to know about the effects of different drugs on the mind and the body.

As a parent, you don't need to have a white lab coat or a badge and a gun in order to feel comfortable and helpful speaking with your kids about drugs.

Parents who are unable to discuss the effects of drugs with their children or who are unwilling to say anything other than "drugs are bad, they'll kill you," may unwittingly force their children to go to other unreliable and dangerous sources to satisfy their curiosity. The children may turn to friends who offer myths and misinformation, or they may be vulnerable to drug dealers who tout the mind-altering potential of drugs as a not-to-be-missed experience. Kids who know they can rely on their parents for straight, believable answers and honest, nonjudgmental discussions are less likely to turn to dangerous experimentation. They will view their parents as credible resources and partners.

Parents, then, should make an effort to understand mood- or mind-altering drugs not as evil substances with magical powers, but as chemicals that interact with our brain's own chemicals to produce physical, psychological, and behavioral effects. And although parents don't need to be walking encyclopedias of pharmacology, they should know what resources to use and where to find such resources when they need information about drugs. This book is a good place to start.

Beyond concern about their children's drug use, parents should also be knowledgeable about the effects of the drugs they themselves use. Whether those drugs are alcohol, caffeine, nicotine, or prescription medicines, parents should be aware of why they use them and how such substances affect their lives.

Keep the channels of communication open. Learn about drug education at your child's school. Watch TV together and talk about the media's portrayal of drug use. Discuss articles and ads in newspapers and magazines. What message or image is being presented? By exploring and learning together, families can develop common attitudes to help avoid many of the abuses associated with drug use.

Mind-Altering or Psychoactive Substances

A drug is a substance other than food that, when taken into the body, changes the functioning of one or more of the body systems. These systems, which are formed by groups of organs working together, control all the body's functions. Drugs are "substances," or chemical compounds, and it is important to note that drugs are not food. Food changes how our body systems function and allows our body to grow and work in a healthy and normal manner. Drugs are substances that have no nutritive value, but they still alter the body's functioning.

The drugs we are focusing on in this book primarily affect the central nervous system. The central nervous system consists of the brain and spinal cord, and is made of billions of nerve cells called neurons. The brain is an electrochemical computer that interprets messages for the rest of our body. It allows us to think, make associations, interpret sensory inputs, and use language; it is also the center of our emotions.

Drugs, when taken into the body by whatever means (swallowing, drinking, inhaling fumes, injecting with a hypodermic needle, smoking, sniffing up the nose, and so on), enter the bloodstream and eventually arrive in the brain. Depending on the type of drug and where in the brain it has its primary action, drugs are capable of producing a large variety of responses in the human nervous system—some pleasant, some disagreeable, some bizarre and unpredictable.

Most people who self-administer drugs do so hoping for a positive experience. Such a response is referred to as a state of intoxication or euphoria, or more commonly by the generic term *high*. In other words, mind-altering chemicals, or drugs that affect the nervous system, can be defined as drugs that get a person high. Other terms associated with drug experiences are *bombed, drunk, stoned, blitzed, toasted, sloshed, smashed, blasted, stupid, wasted, baked, crazy, buzzed,* and *mellow.* Such commonly used terms reflect both the variety of drugs available and the intensity of response based on how much of the drug was used.

To further understand this process, we need to keep in mind that the functioning of the brain is an electrochemical process. The brain has chemicals called neurotransmitters, which are released by electrical charges and convey a variety of messages, such as pleasure, pain, excitement, and relaxation. Mind-altering, or psychoactive, drugs are close in chemical structure to the brain's own natural chemistry, and they act in a way that speeds up, slows down, or substitutes for the brain's normal reactions. That's just about all there is to it.

As you can see, mind-altering substances aren't difficult to understand nor are they "magical." Simply put, they are foreign chemical substances that, when introduced into the body, react with naturally produced chemicals and "play tricks on" or affect the nervous system.

Literally thousands of substances can have a mind-altering or psychoactive effect on the human nervous system. Some occur naturally. They are found in their pure state in nature—most often in plants, but in some cases in minerals and even animals. Some substances are synthetic, the product of a chemist's skill and knowledge, and are manufactured in a laboratory. Some are a combination of natural and synthetic, in that a natural substance is chemically altered by humans to produce a new substance that has psychoactive properties.

The science of psychopharmacology studies the reaction of drugs on the mind. It has greatly advanced our knowledge of how the brain works and has created many useful drugs to treat various mental disorders. But it has also allowed for the synthesis of many drugs of abuse, creating a social problem that will be with us for some time to come.

Classification of Mood-Altering Chemicals

Since thousands of drugs can produce an intoxicating effect on the central nervous system, grouping those drugs according to a system of classification can help us better understand how they work. The easiest system to use classifies drugs in terms of (a) their chemical structure and (b) their primary effect on the central nervous system. Using these guidelines, we can divide all drugs into only three large subgroups: depressants, stimulants, and hallucinogens. Let's briefly describe each subgroup in order to create a framework from which to look at the larger picture of drug use. Then we'll take a look at various drugs under each classification.

Depressants

Drugs in the largest subgroup are known as central nervous system depressants. Depressants are the most common mind-altering drugs, and in many ways they are the most important because they have several medical uses. Since the word *depressant* is related to the verb "to depress," it would be easy to think that anyone who takes a central nervous system depressant would feel gloomy, sad, or down, but the truth is that many people never feel better and more relaxed than when they take depressants.

The term *depressant* refers to the slowing-down effect the drugs have on the central nervous system (a nickname for this group of drugs is "downers"). Because depressants slow down the functioning of the nervous system, they in turn slow down many of the functions of the body. After an initial period of stimulation and intoxication, a person under the influence of a depressant reacts more slowly and talks more slowly than usual. He or she may even have slurred speech. Users have fewer heartbeats and take fewer breaths per minute. If a person takes enough of a depressant drug in a short enough period of time, the body slows down to the point of stopping altogether. Indeed, death from respiratory depression is one of the greatest dangers of depressant drugs.

The most common depressant drug used for mind alteration is alcohol. Yet people rarely think of alcohol as a drug. Nevertheless, it is a very powerful mind-altering drug, and it is also a depressant.

An easy symbol to help us remember the effect of depressants is an arrow pointing downward, like this:

Stimulants

If depressants slow the nervous system down, then stimulants speed the nervous system up. In fact, "speed" and "uppers" are common nicknames for stimulant drugs.

People under the influence of a stimulant are more alert and awake, more nervous and jittery than they would normally be. They find it difficult to sleep and, in some cases, to eat. Most of their body reactions and functions are speeded up; they often talk faster and move more. Their hearts beat faster—sometimes to the point of pounding—and their respiration rates increase. They sweat profusely and are generally restless and agitated. Most stimulants produce similar effects, but they vary in strength and intensity.

With many stimulants, at least initially, a person's mood becomes "elevated." This "high" is the effect others see, but it is short lived. Furthermore, because stimulants drain the body's natural energy over time, many users end up needing them just to reach a normal state of energy. Prolonged stimulant use may make people anxious and even paranoid. Beyond that, each time the effects of the stimulant wear off, an inevitable "down" or depressed feeling ensues. The most commonly available stimulant is caffeine, which is found in coffee beans, tea leaves, cola nuts, and even chocolate. Because caffeine is found in many soft drinks as an artificial additive, children are often introduced to drug use by drinking soda pop. The second most common stimulant is nicotine, a naturally occurring ingredient in tobacco leaves that is available in all forms of tobacco products. Among the more dangerous stimulants are amphetamines (speed) and cocaine.

If we were to use a symbol to help remember the effect of stimulants, we would use an arrow pointing upward:

Hallucinogens

In their natural form, hallucinogens have been known for centuries. American Indians have used and still use hallucinogenic mushrooms (psilocybin) and cactus (mescaline) for religious purposes. Only recently has there been widespread so-called recreational use of hallucinogens in our society. Particularly in the late 1960s and early 1970s, hallucinogenic drugs attracted a lot of media attention because large numbers of young people were experimenting with them for the first time, and the drugs sometimes had bizarre and unpredictable effects on people's perceptions and behavior.

There are two notable aspects of hallucinogens:

1. Even though the word *hallucinogen* has the same root as *hallucination,* most of these drugs do not cause hallucinations. True hallucinations happen when someone sees or hears things that are not there. Most of the effects of hallucinogenic drugs can be called "pseudohallucinations" in that an actual object or sound is perceived, but it is altered or distorted somewhat by the effects of the drug. With higher doses, however, it is possible to get true hallucinations and have a real break with reality, particularly with LSD and PCP. We will have more to say about both of these drugs.

2. Hallucinogens are closely related to stimulants, and they too stimulate the nervous system. Thus, people under the influence of such drugs are usually awake and nervous. They have increased heart and respiration rates, and they sweat heavily. In short, they experience the effects of central nervous system stimulants but with the extra "twist" that hallucinogens cause within the mind. Some extremely powerful hallucinogens, among them many so-called designer drugs, are actually manufactured by taking a stimulant such as methamphetamine and chemically altering it to create a new hallucinogenic drug.

Since there are no recognized medical uses for hallucinogens, they are not available by prescription as are some depressants and stimulants. The most common hallucinogen is marijuana (although some experts think marijuana is unique and should have its own separate classification). Its active ingredient, THC, acts like other hallucinogenic drugs if taken into the body in large enough doses. Since most marijuana has a relatively small percentage of THC, the hallucinogenic effect is not always apparent. Some medical people claim that THC can relieve nausea associated with chemotherapy treatments and may help some glaucoma sufferers as well.

Unlike "downers" or "uppers," we don't have any easy-to-remember nickname for hallucinogens. If we were to use an arrow symbol to represent the effects of these drugs, it might look something like this:

As stated earlier, virtually every drug that can affect the central nervous system falls into one of the above three categories. However, we can't always categorize drugs consistently. Some drugs, such as certain depressants, seem to have paradoxical effects and react one way at first and another way later on. Some seem to "straddle the fence" between two different effects such as those of stimulants and hallucinogens. But in every instance the chemical structure of a drug allows us to place it more accurately in one of the three specific categories.

The most common stimulants and depressants are either completely legal (as is caffeine) or legal once you reach a certain age (as are alcohol and nicotine). Even marijuana has been "decriminalized" in many states, and the penalty for possessing a small amount is equal to the penalty for a traffic violation. Mind-altering drugs are easily available in our society, and sanctions against their use aren't always as great as we may think.

For this reason, it's often said that we live in a drug-oriented society where young people learn at an early age to take a drug when something bothers them or they want to feel better. In our society, children learn that when you get together with people, drugs are often used to enhance the good times. Even the idea of a vitamin pill may give young people the message that taking pills is more important than healthy eating. This is not to say that vitamins aren't "good for you"; but we need to be careful about how we reinforce the behavior of pill taking, for example, by giving kids drugs such as aspirin, cold medication, or other substances in pill form.

Drug Effects: Specific Characteristics of Mind-Altering Chemicals

Physical Dependence or Addiction

Many psychoactive drugs, but particularly depressant drugs, cause physical dependence or addiction. A person is considered physically addicted to a drug when large doses of a drug over a long period of time alter the chemical structure of the individual cells of the nervous system. When addicted persons are cut off from the supply of drugs, either voluntarily or involuntarily, soon after the last dose they exhibit physical symptoms. These physical symptoms are called a "withdrawal syndrome." Depending on the type of drug, the withdrawal varies in length and severity.

Depressant drugs can produce a violent withdrawal reaction in which addicts become extremely physically ill. In the case of heroin, a depressant belonging to the subgroup of opiates, the withdrawal is like the most virulent case of flu imaginable.

Alcohol, another depressant drug, is also physically addicting and can produce severe, even life-threatening withdrawal symptoms. The danger (which also occurs in withdrawal from similar drugs such as barbiturates) is that a person can go into convulsions and seizures and experience cardiac arrest. This is often accompanied by a nightmarelike hallucinogenic state called delirium tremens, or "DT's."

We should not assume that because a drug is legal, it is "safer" than illegal drugs. Alcohol withdrawal can be fatal, whereas heroin withdrawal is nonfatal, yet one is legal and the other completely illegal in the United States. We need to understand all the effects of a drug—even alcohol—before making judgments about how safe it is to use.

Drugs other than depressants can also cause physical addiction and a withdrawal syndrome, but usually they are not as severe or life-threatening as those caused by depressants.

People can even become physically addicted to the relatively "mild" stimulants caffeine and nicotine, and anyone who has tried to quit smoking can attest that for several days the body reacts in all sorts of unpleasant ways. Nicotine withdrawal symptoms include nervousness, sleep disturbance, and in some cases nausea. Caffeine can produce a withdrawal characterized by migrainelike headaches and fatigue. Heavy users of marijuana who quit using the drug may experience a physical withdrawal symptom lasting approximately three days that is characterized by irritability or "crankiness" as well as sleep disturbance.

Tolerance

In order to become physically dependent on a drug, a person must first develop a tolerance to the drug. That is, the person continually needs to increase the amount of a drug in order to obtain the same effect once obtained from a smaller dose.

Take, for example, the reaction of a person who has never before drunk alcohol, as he or she experiments with a six-pack of beer. To the uninitiated nervous system, two or three beers would produce an intoxicating effect (or nausea) that would stop the person from drinking more. If the person in question liked this intoxicating effect, he or she might wish to repeat the experience, and buy a six-pack every weekend. If our new drinker purchased the first six-pack of beer in January, by September or October it might take five or six beers to produce exactly the same effect or "high" that only two or three beers produced a few months earlier.

Our subject is developing a tolerance to the drug ethyl alcohol, and this is the first step on the road to physical addiction. Before a person becomes physically addicted he or she first must be able to consume larger and larger amounts of the drug. In order to do this, the person must develop a tolerance. Sometimes tolerance is developed gradually through steady drinking that increases over time. In youth, tolerance may develop more quickly. Oddly, many adolescents and young adults in our society *brag* about the fact that they have a tolerance. This is particularly true among young males whose ability to "hold their liquor" is a status symbol. Some college fraternities have a ritual called "case day," in which anyone who drinks a whole case of beer of a certain brand is awarded a T-shirt advertising that brand. There is also a game called "quarters," in which a quarter is bounced on a table and into the glass of an opponent who must then drink the entire glass of beer nonstop. Such games have the effect of increasing one's tolerance. In certain peer groups, people who have low tolerance are frowned upon or ridiculed. Not everyone who develops a tolerance eventually becomes physically addicted, but tolerance is a necessary part of that equation. Thus young people who brag about their tolerance are actually taking steps on the road that could lead to physical addiction.

In the case of *cross-tolerance,* a person who has developed tolerance for one drug can have a tolerance to a similar drug without ever introducing that drug into his or her system. For example, a person who has never had a sleeping pill but who has developed a tolerance to alcohol needs more sleeping pills to produce a sedative effect on the nervous system than if he or she had never drunk. Cross-tolerance can also be seen when withdrawal symptoms from one drug are relieved by taking a different but similar drug.

Physiological "facts of life" such as cross-tolerance demonstrate all too graphically that when people alter their minds with drugs, they dangerously interfere with the biochemical structure of their brains. Potentially, drug use may cause changes in behavior and thinking that are hard to reverse.

Overdose

A person overdoses on a drug when he or she introduces too much of the substance into the system and it becomes toxic or poisonous to the body. It is possible to overdose on virtually any drug; all legally manufactured drugs supply product information concerning signs and symptoms of overdose as well as steps to follow for emergency medical care.

In the case of some drugs, the symptoms of overdose are relatively mild and pass quickly as the drug naturally "wears off" and is pharmacologically eliminated from the body. An overdose of depressants, however, is particularly dangerous because of the drugs' slowing-down effect on the nervous system. It is easier to die from an overdose of a depressant than from almost any other type of drug. To understand how this can happen, we need to be familiar with two fairly simple concepts: the "dose-response ratio" and the "synergistic effect."

Dose-Response Ratio

Those who remember their junior high math know that a ratio expresses a relationship between two numbers, and in the dose-response ratio the two numbers in question are expressed like this:

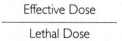

Effective Dose

Lethal Dose

The effective dose of a drug refers to the amount of the drug necessary to produce a noticeable effect on the nervous system. In the example of alcohol, the effective dose would be a one and one-half ounce "shot" of 86 proof liquor (for example, whiskey, brandy, vodka, gin, or rum), a five-ounce glass of wine, or a twelve-ounce can of beer.

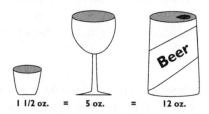

1 1/2 oz.　=　5 oz.　=　12 oz.

A short time after ingesting an effective dose of alcohol—the minimum amount needed to produce a noticeable effect—the drinker feels somewhat light-headed or relaxed. This state is not to be confused with being drunk. "Drunk" is legally defined by each state. In most states this means a person's blood alcohol content (BAC) is 0.10 percent. It takes the average adult male about four and one-half times the effective dose to reach this legal level.

The above effective dose of alcohol would be expressed as a "1" in the top number of the ratio:

$$\frac{1}{\text{Lethal Dose}}$$

The bottom number for the lethal dose of alcohol would be "12" or twelve times that amount ingested in the same period of time:

$$\frac{1}{12}$$

That is, if one shot of liquor, glass of wine, or can of beer produces an effect, then twelve drinks of equal amount ingested in an hour or less would prove fatal to about 50 percent of the population (what scientists call the LD50). In the case of liquor, eighteen ounces (or a little more than a pint) would cause someone to pass out and become comatose. In the case of wine (sixty ounces or about a half-gallon in an hour) or beer (a whole twelve-pack), it is more difficult to achieve a lethal overdose; but remember that this number applies to a 160-pound adult. For a younger, smaller person, it takes less alcohol. Thus, alcohol is a particularly dangerous drug for young people, because it is often the drug that is the easiest to obtain. Furthermore, children and early adolescents (ten to twelve years of age) are the ones who most often attempt naive or uninformed experimentation and risk death by overdose.

In some respects, the ratio can be looked upon as a "margin of safety." Most depressants, because they slow down the heart beat and respiration rate, either have ratios similar to the alcohol ratio or have effective and lethal doses somewhat closer to one another. With certain drugs used for cancer chemotherapy, the safety margin is so small that the difference between the effective dose and the lethal dose is almost nil; such drugs must be administered under constant medical supervision. Conversely, the ratio with other drugs, as some hallucinogens, is one to several thousand. Death by overdose is not the major concern, but other problems associated with those drugs make use of them worrisome.

1 + 1 = 5: Synergy, a Sneaky Death

The synergistic effect, which greatly increases the risk of overdose, is a concept that merits understanding. With synergy 1 + 1 equals 3 or 4 or even 5!

Certain drugs, particularly depressants, when mixed or taken in combination, multiply the other's effects. Many drugs are metabolized (broken down into components the body can use) in the liver by chemicals called enzymes. Specific enzymes act on certain types of drugs. Because many depressants are similar to one another in chemical structure, it is possible for all the appropriate enzymes to be busy breaking down one drug. When a similar one enters the system, it can go into the blood-stream in a relatively undiluted form, thereby multiplying its effect on the body and the brain.

Alcohol, when mixed with drugs such as barbiturates or other sedatives, can be deadly. This lethal combination causes more deaths by overdose, either accidental or deliberate, than any other drug. This synergistic effect can be "sneaky" and, as in the case of alcohol and some cold medicines, unexpected.

It is also possible to overdose on drugs other than depressants. In the case of stimulants such as amphetamines or cocaine, a lethal overdose can take the form of a cardiac arrhythmia, a reaction that is analogous to a car engine that falters and quits after being over-revved at a high speed. Overdose is a very real danger with drug use and can often prove fatal; it's something anyone thinking about drug use should consider.

Psychological Dependence

Psychological dependence is the last characteristic of mind-altering chemicals that we will discuss in this section. A person who is *physically* dependent is addicted to the drug; a person who is *psychologically* dependent is addicted to the "high" that the drug produces.

What drug users interpret as a high is actually a reduction in anxiety or depression and a temporary boost in the ability to "have fun." Drug users who experience artificial self-esteem provided by chemical highs may find the return to the real world painful—and to be avoided at all costs.

Psychologically dependent people fall in love with the intoxicating effects of "their" drug and think they can't make it through the day without a lift. Although this mental craving or "drug hunger" and genuine physical addiction differ, psychological dependence can be every bit as stubborn to overcome as physical addiction. A person who is psychologically "hooked" will often beg, borrow, or steal to obtain his or her drug. Such a person will not, however, experience the excruciating illness of withdrawal unless his or her body is physically addicted as well. This withdrawal will force the addict to extremes, whereas those with an exclusively psychological habit can eventually go to sleep without the extreme discomfort and pain of the physical addict.

The relationship between physical and psychological addiction is that most people who eventually take enough of a drug to become physically addicted are first psychologically addicted. After all, why do people keep putting a drug in their mouths or up their noses or into their veins or down their lungs? The answer: they are psychologically hooked on the high. This form of drug dependence is insidious. When people have too much of their identities tied up in the drug subculture, it can destroy family relationships, friendships, and job performances and lead to financial, legal, and psychological difficulties. To such people, obtaining a high becomes so important it distorts their sense of reality. As a result, sometimes it is difficult to determine who is more "hooked"—the physical drug addict or the person who has developed a "psychological habit."

So be aware that although true physical addiction with severe withdrawal symptoms is mainly the result of depressant drugs, use of any intoxicating drug—depressant, stimulant, or hallucinogen—can cause psychological dependence.

Drug Information Tables

The following pages provide a quick reference guide to the different types of depressants, stimulants, and hallucinogens. Subgroups or individual drugs are included under each major category, along with common nicknames, major characteristics, harmful effects, and prognoses.

Depressants

Drug: Alcohol (Ethyl Alcohol)

Common forms of alcohol are beer, wine, and distilled spirits such as whiskey, vodka, gin, brandy, and schnapps.

Nicknames: Brew, grape, booze, hootch, juice, sauce.

Characteristics: A legal, socially acceptable depressant drug used by about 70 percent of the adult population. In small doses it causes relaxation and increases sociability. In large doses it slows down the body's reaction time, decreases coordination, slurs speech, and can make the user uninhibited or belligerent.

Harmful Effects: In the short term, alcohol can cause the user to black out, pass out, become nauseated, and feel terribly "hung over." It can cause psychological dependence as well as physical addiction with dangerous withdrawal, including delirium tremens. The user develops a rapid tolerance and can overdose as well. Alcohol interferes with the healthy functioning of the heart, liver, kidney, and stomach. Pregnant women can pass the debilitating fetal alcohol syndrome on to their babies. In the United States, about 100,000 people die from the effects of alcohol abuse every year.

Alcohol is associated with many social problems, including loss of job productivity, domestic violence, and violent crime. Drunk driving continues to be a major cause of traffic deaths.

Prognosis: Alcohol will continue to be our number one drug problem unless people set clear standards about appropriate alcohol use and learn how it affects them personally. Strict rules about drinking and driving are necessary, and all adults need to be aware of the examples they set for children.

Drug: Sedatives

Sedatives include (a) barbiturates such as Seconal, Tuinal, and Phenobarbitol and (b) other prescription sleeping pills such as Doriden and Methaqualone (Quaaludes).

Nicknames: Downers, barbs, goofballs, reds, red devils, rainbows, stumblers, ludes, soaps, disco biscuits.

Characteristics: Medically used in pill form to induce sleep, sedatives have a relaxing effect similar to alcohol. Users typically exhibit slurred speech, slower body responses and movement, and sloppy, mawkish behavior. They often end up passing out or blacking out.

Harmful Effects: Like alcohol, sedatives can cause tolerance and both psychological and physical addiction, with life-threatening withdrawal. Overdose is common, and death often occurs when sedatives are mixed with alcohol (see Synergy, page 120). When prescribed for insomnia, they create an artificial "stupor" and interfere with the body's natural sleep cycle. As a result, users feel tired rather than refreshed when they awaken.

Prognosis: Although sedatives are not currently "in vogue," there is always a danger of their being rediscovered by a new population of potential drug abusers. They will probably continue to be legally manufactured and prescribed as long as our society is worried about getting a "good night's sleep" and think that the way to obtain it is through drug use.

Drug: Minor Tranquilizers (Anxiolytics)

Minor tranquilizers include (a) benzodiazepines such as Librium, Valium, Ativan, and the newcomers Xanax and Halcion and (b) meprobamates (Miltown, Equanil, and Deprol).

Nicknames: Downers, tranks, nerve pills, the "housewife's drug."

Characteristics: Minor tranquilizers such as Valium are medically prescribed to reduce anxiety (and as muscle relaxants), and they seem to make the stresses and strains of everyday living almost "magically" melt away. They were, for this reason, the most overprescribed drugs of the 1960s and 1970s. Besides reducing anxiety, they flatten all emotional responses, so it is often hard for users to know how they feel about anything.

Harmful Effects: Tolerance, physical addiction, and psychological dependence are a danger with these drugs. The danger of overdose is particularly strong if these drugs are mixed with alcohol. A large percentage of addicts are women, reflecting the prescribing practices of the medical profession.

Prognosis: Abuse of these drugs has greatly declined in recent years, largely because the medical profession has recognized the practice of overprescribing minor tranquilizers and is setting stricter guidelines for their use.

Drug: Narcotic Analgesics

Narcotic analgesics include (a) opiates (derived from the opium poppy) such as heroin (the strongest), morphine, and codeine (weakest) and (b) synthetic forms of morphine, such as Demerol, Dilaudid, and Methadone.

Nicknames: "H," "M," horse, smack, dope, junk, narc, speedball (when mixed with cocaine).

Characteristics: Medically used as pain relievers, these drugs typically produce a dreamy, relaxed, euphoric state in the user. They are often injected intravenously, and street heroin is heavily diluted with inert white powders such as lactose.

Harmful Effects: These are among the most physically addicting of all drugs, with the user acquiring a rapid tolerance. Because they are often injected, there is a great danger of passing AIDS and other diseases through contaminated needles. They also present one of the greatest risks of death by overdose because of the extreme respiratory depression and shallow breathing that can result from doses not much greater than the effective dose. Narcotic addiction holds addicts in a very tight grip because of the painful withdrawal; such users often turn to crime to obtain money to satisfy the craving.

Prognosis: The popularity of heroin as a street drug declined with the advent of cocaine and crack, but it appears to be making a comeback in some cities.

Drug: Inhalants

Inhalants include the fumes of common household and volatile industrial substances such as paint, glue, gasoline, paint thinner, and other petroleum products; aerosol products such as hair spray, shoe polish, and room deodorants; typewriter correction fluid; and amyl and butyl nitrite.

Nicknames: Gas, glue, snappers, poppers, locker room, rush.

Characteristics: The fumes of these substances are inhaled (huffed) for effects somewhat akin to alcohol or other depressants, with "side attractions" of dizziness, giddiness, and hallucinations.

Harmful Effects: Inhalants are mainly substances that were never intended to be used for a "high." The hydrocarbon compounds that produce the "high" effect can cause harm to a number of the body's organ systems, including liver damage, kidney failure, respiratory difficulty, digestive disorders, and heart irregularities. Death from suffocation can be unpredictable and swift. Toluene, the substance in model airplane glue, can cause permanent damage to the nervous system. Inhalant abuse is one of the most dangerous forms of drug use.

Prognosis: Young people are particularly susceptible to inhalants because of their easy availability. Many communities now have anti-inhalant "projects" to educate young people about the dangers of the inhalants.

Stimulants

Drug: Caffeine

Caffeine occurs naturally in coffee beans, tea leaves, cola nuts, and cocoa beans. It is an artificial additive in 95 percent (by volume) of soft drinks sold in the United States. Sold over the counter in pill form (NoDoz, Vivarin).

Nicknames: Mud, java, bean, pop, speed, zip, wakeup.

Characteristics: Caffeine in the most common of all drugs, and it is completely legal. It is introduced to very young children through soft drinks. It produces a mild stimulating effect in which the user becomes more alert, awake, and focused.

Harmful Effects: Caffeine can produce nervousness, anxiety, insomnia, irritability, and disturbances in heart rate and rhythm. It can increase blood pressure and secretion of stomach acid. Users develop a rapid tolerance and can become physically addicted. The condition called "caffeinism" can occur when a person drinks at least four to six cups of coffee a day (a minimum of 250 mg of caffeine). Withdrawal is characterized by severe headaches and fatigue.

Prognosis: Despite the problems, caffeine will probably remain legal and easy to get. People are more frequently choosing caffeine-free beverages because of the drug's harmful effects.

Drug: Nicotine

Nicotine is a stimulant found in tobacco leaves and therefore all tobacco products, including cigarettes, cigars, and smokeless tobacco products (snuff).

Nicknames: Cigs, butts, smokes, coffin nails, squares, chew, dip.

Characteristics: Nicotine is a legal, highly addictive stimulant most commonly used through cigarette smoking. As a stimulant it first causes an increase in heart rate, blood pressure, and respiration rate. These effects are followed by a brief period of relaxation, with improved concentration, alertness, and "focus." The typical cigarette smoker takes one or two puffs per minute. About two hours after the last cigarette, a craving for another one sets in.

Harmful Effects: Nicotine is the number one killer drug in our society, with one out of seven deaths being tobacco related (360,000 annually in the United States and 2.5 million worldwide). Most deaths are caused by lung diseases, but mouth cancers are increasing because of the spread of smokeless tobacco use. Smoking by pregnant women often causes lower birth weight in babies, and there is increased evidence of the harmful effects of secondhand smoke. Despite these hazards, consumers spend $30 billion a year on tobacco products because they are so addictive. The strong physical addiction caused by nicotine creates unpleasant withdrawal symptoms such as nervousness, agitation, craving, extreme testiness, and sleep disturbance.

Prognosis: Despite the $1 billion spent on advertising each year, the number of smokers has been cut in half, from 50 to 25 percent of the adult population. There is a strong movement for smoke-free workplaces and buildings used by the public. Virtually everyone is aware of the health hazards of cigarette smoking, but because of the addiction factor, we may always have some tobacco users.

Drug: Amphetamines

The powerful central nervous system stimulants known as amphetamines include (a) amphetamine sulphate (Benzedrine), (b) dextromphetamine sulphate (Dexedrine), and (c) methamphetamine hydrochloride (Methedrine).

Nicknames: Speed, crank, zip, bennies, dexies, meth, wide-eye, ice.

Characteristics: Amphetamines are among the most powerful stimulants. They can be taken in pill form, snorted, injected, or smoked as in the case of "ice." People on amphetamines are alert, awake, vigorous, talkative, hyperattentive, sociable, and anorexic. These effects last for several hours and are followed by anxiety, nausea, weakness, and depression as the drug wears off. Amphetamines were once commonly prescribed for weight control but are now used mainly for narcolepsy and attention deficit disorder in children.

Harmful Effects: Amphetamines can be extremely psychologically addicting (frequent users are sometimes called "speed freaks"). Prolonged use causes extreme anorexia, and psychoticlike conditions with anxiety, paranoia, hallucinations, and repetitive compulsive behavior. Death by overdose is possible. Other risks include malnutrition, disease, and dangers from injection.

Prognosis: There was recently a fear of an "ice" epidemic because of the availability of this smokable from of methamphetamine. This epidemic never occurred, probably because the punishing effects of amphetamines on the mind and body make their use largely self-limiting.

Drug: Cocaine

Cocaine refers to both "regular" cocaine hydrochloride and the smokable freebase form commonly known as crack.

Nicknames: Coke, blow, toot, snow, white powder, flake, lady, "C," crack, rock.

Characteristics: A white, crystalline powder extracted from the leaves of the South American coca bush. When inhaled up the nose ("snorted"), it is absorbed through the mucous membrane and produces a feeling of increased energy, alertness, and well-being that lasts about a half hour at its peak. The user then has a strong compulsion to repeat the dose. Cocaine in this form is expensive (about $100 a gram) and is often diluted with inert powders ("cut" or "stepped on"). Crack is a purified from of the drug that is "smoked" (melted at a high temperature in a glass pipe and the vapors inhaled). This way of taking the drug delivers a powerful dose directly to the brain, and the "high" is much more intense and shorter lasting than when the drug is snorted, bringing out much more compulsive behavior in the user.

Harmful Effects: Continued use can create a strong psychological dependence with physical overtones. This dependence eventually can produce a depressed, paranoid, almost psychotic state similar to that brought on by amphetamines. Overdose can result in death by cardiac arrest. Use by pregnant women has resulted in "cocaine babies" who display a variety of abnormalities. Prolonged use can also produce "coke bugs," or the sensation of crawling insects just beneath the surface of the skin.

Prognosis: As long as there are tremendous profits from illicit cocaine traffic, the drug will continue to be smuggled into the United States. Use by young people has declined recently, partly owing to the success of public information campaigns educating youth about the devastating effects of crack.

Hallucinogens

Drug: LSD (d-lysergic acid diethylamide)

Nicknames: Acid, cid, sydney, blotter, microdot, window pane, green pyramids, other "brand names."

Characteristics: LSD is one of the most powerful drugs known to humanity, in that the dose is measured in micrograms (.000001 gram). One hundred micrograms when swallowed can result in a hallucinogenic "trip" lasting ten to twelve hours. LSD powerfully disrupts sensory inputs and thought processes, and can cause tremendous changes in the emotional state of the user. At larger doses (more than 250 micrograms) the user can experience true hallucinations and see or hear things that are not there.

Harmful Effects: Adverse reactions known as "bum trips" or "bummers" are fairly common. A person experiencing a bummer may have repetitive nightmarish thought patterns or paranoid feelings that people are out to get him or her. There may be a panic reaction or "freakout" requiring medical attention. LSD can bring out latent psychological problems and cause strong personality changes, dangerous delusional behavior such as attempting to fly, or even suicide. "Flashbacks" can also occur in which the former user experiences a repeat of the LSD experience days and even months after the drug was taken.

Prognosis: LSD is making a comeback in popularity among young people, but it is taken as a "party drug" in doses of fifty to one hundred micrograms, smaller than the doses taken in the sixties and seventies. Use among high school seniors has increased for the first time in several years.

Drug: PCP (Phencyclidine)

Nicknames: Peace pill, angel dust, dust, crystal, "T," THC, cannibinol, crank, hog, goon, zoot, embalming fluid, rocket fuel. Marijuana treated with PCP has been called supergrass or killer weed, and the individual cigarettes referred to as Shermans or Sherms.

Characteristics: PCP is more accurately called a disassociative anesthetic. It was widely used for a time as an animal tranquilizer. The drug can be swallowed in pill or liquid form, sniffed, injected, or put on a leafy plant substance and smoked. The effects are strongly dose related, with low-dose users reporting a mild euphoria. As the dose increases, so do feelings of subjective detachment, and at high doses it is possible to have complete breaks with reality, with manic and schizophreniclike states, and agitated or violent behavior. Because of its well-deserved negative reputation, PCP has been remarketed under more different nicknames than any other drug.

Harmful Effects: Because of difficulty in controlling dose size, more people have severe reactions to PCP than to any other hallucinogen. It is also possible to overdose on PCP. The result is a catatonic state with grimacing and mute behavior or grandiose delusions, hallucinations, and complete depersonalization. Prolonged use takes a heavy toll on the nervous system, and a feeling of "burnout" is a commonly reported symptom among heavy users.

Prognosis: As long as there is an illicit underground drug scene, PCP will most likely be around. Its continued use is due partly to the ease of manufacture of the drug and partly to its bizarre effects, which bring out the "thrill seeker" in a certain type of drug abuser. Luckily, the well-deserved bad reputation of PCP has limited its use to only a small percentage of the drug culture.

Drug: Marijuana

The marijuana family includes regular marijuana (leaves and flower tops of "seeded" female plants), sinsemilla (highly potent seedless, unfertilized flower tops of the female plant), and hashish or hash (compressed resin gathered from flower tops).

Nicknames: Pot, weed, reefer, herb, boo, grass, rope; bud, skunk bud, sticky bud; sinsey, sense (nicknames for sinsemilla); ganja, Thaistick, Maui wowie.

Characteristics: Marijuana is a large weedy plant that grows throughout the world. Dried marijuana is usually rolled into cigarettes (joints or doobies) or smoked in small pipes (bowls or pinch hitters) or large cylindrical devices (bongs). The "high" lasts one to four hours and can range from mild euphoria, relaxation, or giddiness to a depersonalized "spaced out" feeling. Strong doses can produce a subhallucinogenic state, with paranoia and a panic reaction somewhat like that caused by other hallucinogens.

Harmful Effects: Because marijuana is smoked, there is evidence of decreased functioning of the lungs in regular users. Marijuana smoke also contains cancer-causing particles. Regular marijuana use may temporarily decrease the body's ability to fight infection. It also lowers levels of the male hormone testosterone, which may lead to increased breast development in males.

It is well documented that marijuana affects short-term memory and interferes with the ability to concentrate. Users have a poor sense of time and space, and this effect interferes with the ability to drive and perform other complex tasks. It also affects adolescents' ability to learn. In fact, teenage users often lose interest in school or anything else that doesn't involve marijuana use.

Prognosis: Marijuana use among high school seniors has steadily declined since 1979, but there are still about two million users in the United States, mainly adolescents and young adults. Adolescents are particularly vulnerable to the strong marijuana (sinsemilla) available today. Many who use the drug regularly continue to get stuck in a self-indulgent, pleasure-seeking dead end, unable to demonstrate any consistent maturity or responsibility.

Chemical Use Continuum

Different people exhibit different behaviors in relation to the drugs just discussed. These relationships are easily seen when we look at all drug use on a continuum. By definition, a continuum is a continuous line on which everything or everyone that is being measured falls. The following continuum defines five "benchmark" behaviors relating to chemical use and shows how one leads into the next.

It is important to note that the chemical use continuum is a two-way street, and it is possible for people to move back and forth on it by changing their behavior. Change is most difficult at the dependence end, and this is why treatment is most often necessary at that level of use.

Activity—Chemical Use Self-Assessment

Everyone reading this book can place himself or herself somewhere on the chemical use continuum. Think about your own behavior in light of the definitions above, and

1. Place a dot indicating where you are now, in the past three months.

2. Place a dot indicating where you were at the heaviest point of use in your life (for example, in high school or college).

If your two dots are in about the same place, what does that say? If there is a distance between your dots, what changes have you made in your life to cause this?

The point of this type of self-assessment is to examine behaviors and make any adjustments necessary to avoid harm or problems in the future. Share the continuum with family members. Take any steps necessary to move left on the continuum.

Chemical Use Continuum

Abstinence (selective)

The choice not to use mood-altering chemicals. This usually means alcohol or illegal drugs; caffeine and nicotine are often used. About 35 percent of the adult population.

Social Use

Legal, socially acceptable, "normal" use. Alcohol is the drug of choice in Western society. Examples include having wine with dinner or having friends over for beer and a TV football game. The drug doesn't always have to be alcohol, depending on the culture (peyote, a hallucinogen, is used in religious rituals in a socially acceptable manner among American Indians).

Misuse

Any use that is "harmful"—where there is actual harm or the potential for harm either to the person using or to other people. Harm can be physical or emotional. Examples include getting drunk and picking fights, being verbally abusive, or getting into sexual situations that are later regretted.

Abuse

Planned and chronic misuse of chemicals. Abusers are people who must "party" in order to have fun and do so in a regular, predictable manner. Problems develop in different areas: school or work, family, friends, finances, legal, psychological, and physical.

Dependence

Compulsive, uncontrollable abuse, despite the harmful consequences. The dependent person will either deny the existence of problems or will try to control abuse but be unable to. It usually requires treatment and abstinence to arrest the condition. About 7 to 10 percent of everyone who uses.

Glossary

Alcohol: A legal depressant drug, used as a beverage in many forms, and the most widely used "high" producing drug in our society.

Drug: Any substance other than food that when taken into the body changes the functioning of one or more of the body's systems.

Mind-altering or psychoactive drug: A drug that has its primary effect is on the central nervous system and that changes the thought processes, sensory perceptions, or emotional state of the user.

Prevention: The sum total of knowledge, skills, and attitudes necessary to minimize the impact of alcohol and other drugs on the individual, the family, and society.

Recovery: The lifelong process whereby the alcohol- or drug-dependent person maintains sobriety and learns living and coping skills. This process usually involves regular participation in a self-help group such as Alcoholics Anonymous (AA).

Treatment: The therapeutic process prescribed to anyone who has become physically or psychologically dependent on alcohol or other drugs. It usually involves education, individual and group counseling, and family therapy, with abstinence a common goal.

Research and Further Reading

Books

Black, Claudia. *It Will Never Happen to Me!* Denver: M.A.C. Printing and Publications Division, 1981.

Bozarth-Campbell, Alla, Ph.D. *Life Is Goodbye, Life Is Hello.* Minneapolis: CompCare Publications, 1982.

Clarke, Jean Illsley, et al. *Help! For Parents of Children from Birth to Five.* San Francisco: HarperSanFrancisco, 1993.

———. *Help! For Parents of School-Age Children and Teenagers.* San Francisco: HarperSanFrancisco, 1993.

———. *Self-Esteem: A Family Affair.* San Francisco: Harper & Row, 1978.

Clarke, Jean Illsley, and Dawson, Connie. *Growing Up Again: Parenting Ourselves, Parenting Our Children.* San Francisco: HarperCollins, 1989. Center City, MN: Hazelden Educational Materials, 1989.

Heegaard, Marge Eaton. *Coping with Death and Grief.* Minneapolis: Lerner Publication Company, 1990.

Kubler-Ross, Elisabeth. *Questions and Answers on Death and Dying.* New York: Macmillan, 1974.

Levin, Pamela. *Becoming the Way We Are.* Deerfield Beach, FL: Health Communications, 1988.

Quinsey, Mary Beth. *Why Does That Man Have Such a Big Nose?* Seattle: Parenting Press, 1986.

Ray, Dr. Oakley, and Ksir, Dr. Charles. *Drug Society and Human Behavior.* St. Louis: Times Mirror–Mosby College Publishing, 1987.

Rosenberg, Ellen. *Growing Up Feeling Good.* New York: Viking Penguin Books, 1989.

Wegscheider-Cruse, Sharon. *Choice Making.* Deerfield Beach, FL: Health Communications, 1987.

Booklets and Pamphlets

"Alcohol: Choices and Guidelines for College Students." Saint Paul, MN: Health Promotion Resources, 1990.

DIN Publications, Phoenix. Series of booklets and pamphlets on specific drugs of abuse, 1987.

"Steroids and Our Students: A Guide for Parents." Sturgis, MI: WBA Ruster Foundation.

Svendsen, Roger, and Tom Griffin. "Choices and Influences" series: "Choosing not to Use Alcohol: Benefits for Adolescents"; "Setting Guidelines for Choices About Alcohol"; "What to Say, What to Do: When Someone's Alcohol or Other Drug Use Concerns You." Saint Paul, MN and Sturgis, MI: Health Promotion Resources and WBA Ruster Foundation, 1990.

Curricula

Horizons, Summit Center Drug Abuse Prevention Program. Summit Center for Human Development, 6 Hospital Plaza, Clarksburg, WV 26301 (304-623-5661), 1987.

Project Charlie, Drug Abuse Prevention Program. 4570 W. 77th St., Edina, MN 55435 (1-800-279-KIDS). A program of Storefront Youth Action, 1992.

Other Learning Materials

Books

Affirmation Ovals: 139 Ways to Give and Get Affirmations, by Jean Illsley Clarke and Carole Gesme.

Help for Kids! Understanding Your Feelings About Having a Parent in Prison/Jail, by Carole Gesme.

Help for Kids! Understanding Your Feelings About Moving, by Carole Gesme.

Help for Kids! Understanding Your Feelings About War, by Carole Gesme.

Ouch! That Hurts, A Handbook for People Who Hate Criticism, by Jean Illsley Clarke.

Affirmations

Affirmation Ovals in English or Spanish.

Games by Carole Gesme

Keyed Up for Being Drug Free. Eight years through adult. (A game based on this book.)

Love Game: A Pathway out of Shame into Celebration. Eight years through adult.

Ups & Downs with Feelings Game. Three to six years.

Capture a Feeling. Card game for six years through adult.

Ups & Downs with Feelings Game. Six years through adult.

Additional Tools by Carole Gesme

Feeling Faces Paper People

Feeling Faces Stickers (thirty-six faces)

Laminated Feeling Faces Board (18" × 12")

Pink Permission Messages

Self-Esteem Calendar for Kids

Audio Cassette Tapes: Developmental Stories by Jean Illsley Clarke

"The Important Infants"

"The Wonderful Busy Ones"

"The Terrific Twos"

Newsletter

WE, A Newsletter for People Who Care About Self-Esteem

For information contact:
Carole Gesme
4036 Kerry Court
Minnetonka, MN 55345
or
Daisy Press
16535 9th Avenue N.
Minneapolis, MN 55447

Research

This *Help! For Kids and Parents About Drugs* book is the result of the authors' experiences in prevention, as parents and as professionals, and of the research conducted by the authors and by others. As a result of this research, *we believe that parents are the single most important influence in their children's life regarding drug use.*

Research evidence supports the following conclusions:

- Children need parents to model consistent healthy behavior and attitudes about drug use.
- Children need parents to teach direct drug information and skills that will help young people resist outside influences to use drugs.
- Children and families need the support of the community to complete the prevention effort.

There have been many significant studies on drug use, abuse, and prevention. Throughout the book we credit research sources when we have used them directly. We recognize that many of the same ideas have been explored by other researchers as well.

1. (Brown U.) *Family Systems Medicine,* vol. 8, pp. 191–200 (1990). This research was quoted in *Brown University Child and Adolescent Behavior Letter.*

2. (Farris/Jones) "Ethanol Metabolism in Male American Indians and Whites," by J. J. Farris and B. M. Jones. *Clinical and Experimental Research,* vol. 2, no. 1, pp. 77–81 (1978).

3. (MIPH) *Lessons Learned: An Update on Research in Drug Education,* by the Minnesota Institute of Public Health, 1989, pp. 1–32.

   This project profiles the most current research to assist schools in understanding the limits as well as the possibilities of drug education. The principal author is Jerry Jaker, Ed.S., executive director of the Minnesota Institute of Public Health. Quoted data on prevalence of alcoholism in families with a history of abuse came from Jerry Jaker in private conversations in 1992.

4. (MSSR) *Minnesota Student Survey Report.* Minnesota State Department of Education, 1989.

   The survey was administered to 91,175 students in grades six, nine, and twelve from 390 of Minnesota's 433 public school districts. Its purpose was to identify young people at risk and to investigate health-related problems and concerns among young people.

5. (NIAAA) *Biological and Genetic Factors in Alcoholism.* Research Monograph 9. Rockville, MD: National Institute on Alcohol Abuse and Alcoholism, 1983.

6. (Search Institute) *The Troubled Journey: A Portrait of 6th–12th Grade Youth.* Minneapolis: Search Institute, 1993.

   Developed by Dr. Peter L. Benson, president of Search Institute in Minneapolis, this nationwide survey has been administered to nearly 47,000 students from public schools in 111 communities in twenty-five states. This nationwide effort is aimed at helping parents, schools, youth-serving agencies, congregations, and communities work together in promoting positive youth development.

7. (Stinnett/DeFrain) *Secrets of Strong Families,* by Nick Stinnett and John DeFrain. New York: Berkeley Books, 1985.

This extensive research project surveyed strong families and identified the six characteristics they shared: (1) time together, (2) positive communication, (3) skill handling grief and tragedy, (4) spiritual commitment, (5) commitment to each other, and (6) complimenting each other.

8. (USDHHS) *Adolescent Peer Pressure, Theory Correlates, and Program Implications for Drug Abuse Prevention,* developed by the U.S. Department of Health and Human Services, Public Health Service and Alcohol, Drug Abuse, and Mental Health Administration, 1988, pp. 13–18, 30, 31.

This empirically based research provides evidence of factors associated with drug abuse and other forms of problem behavior.

9. (Wolin et al.) "Disrupted Family Rituals: A Factor in the Intergenerational Transmission of Alcoholism," by Steven J. Wolin, M.D., Linda H. Bennett, Ph.D., Denise L. Noonan, and Martha A. Teitelbaum, M.P.H. *Journal of Studies on Alcohol,* vol. 41, no. 3 (1980), pp. 201, 202.

Where to Go for Additional Support

The following organizations are available to help parents and young people with information about drug abuse prevention and other drug issues. We only give a partial list of the resources available to you. We encourage you to consult your local organizations, libraries, schools, and community service agencies for more information. Many of the national organizations listed have local offices in your city (check the white pages in your phone book). Since the way in which these resources are presented may vary from one locale to another, you may wish to try several of them to find the resource that best meets your needs.

Information

Center for Substance Abuse Prevention (CSAP), Rockville, MD, 301-443-0373.

National AIDS Hot Line, 1-800-342-AIDS.

National Association for Children of Alcoholics, South Laguna, CA, 301-468-0985.

National Clearing House for Alcohol and Drug Information (NCADI), Rockville, MD, 301-468-2600.

National Federation of Parents for Drug-Free Youth, Inc., St. Louis, MO, 314-845-1933.

National Institute on Alcohol Abuse and Alcoholism (NIAAA), Scientific Communications Branch, Rockville, MD, 301-443-3860.

National Institute on Drug Abuse (NIDA), Rockville, MD, 800-729-6686.

National PTA Drug and Alcohol Abuse Prevention Project, Chicago, IL, 312-787-0977.

Office on Smoking and Health, Rockville, MD, 301-443-1575.

Parents for Drug-Free Youth, Silver Spring, MD, 800-662-HELP.

PRIDE, Atlanta, GA, 404-577-4500.

Support and Programs

Al-Anon Family Group Headquarters, New York, NY, 800-344-2666.

Alcoholics Anonymous, New York, NY, 212-870-3400.

Children Are People Support Groups, Inc., St. Paul, MN, 612-490-9257.

Families in Action, Decatur, GA, 404-231-8794.

Hazelden Foundation, Center City, MN, 800-328-9000.

Institute on Black Chemical Abuse, Minneapolis, MN, 612-871-7878.

Johnson Institute, Minneapolis, MN, 800-231-5165.

Mothers Against Drunk Driving (MADD), Hurst, TX, 214-744-6233.

Parent Communication Network (PCN), Apple Valley, MN, 612-432-2886.

Project Charlie, Drug Abuse Prevention Curriculum and Family Prevention Program, Edina, MN, 612-830-1432 or 800-279-KIDS.

Students Against Drunk Driving (SADD), Marlboro, MA, 800-521-SADD.

How to Lead a Suggestion Circle

The Suggestion Circle is a technique for collecting ideas. It is the opposite of brainstorming. Use it to tap the wisdom of a group. As the leader:

1. Ask eight to twelve people to sit in a circle.

2. Ask the person with a problem to state one problem in one or two sentences and then listen.

3. Ask someone else to make a written list of the suggestions so the listener can give full attention to listening.

4. Contract with the listener to accept each suggestion with no comment other than "thank you."

5. Ask the people in the Suggestion Circle to think carefully for a minute about possible solutions to the problem and then have each person give one high-quality, one-or-two-sentence ("You could . . . " or "I would . . . ") suggestion. They are to go in order around the circle and are not to comment on or evaluate each other's suggestions. People in the circle have a right to pass.

6. When the suggestions have been given, remind the listener to take the list home and decide which suggestions to use.

You can do a telephone circle by calling six people and asking each for two possible solutions to your problem.

Index

Index

About the Authors

Donald Brundage has been a social studies teacher, alcohol and drug abuse counselor, and chemical awareness coordinator in a number of school districts in the Minnesota Twin Cities area since 1971. He has spoken to hundreds of families about drugs and drug use prevention over the past ten years. He holds B.A. and B.S. degrees and a master of arts in education.

Jean Illsley Clarke is the author of *Self-Esteem: A Family Affair* and coauthor of *Growing Up Again* and the *Help! for Parents* books. She is a nationally certified family life educator and leads workshops internationally. She holds a master of arts in human development and an honorary doctorate in Human Services.

Carole Gesme, holds a master of arts in human development and is a certified chemical dependency counselor, a prevention specialist, an author of children's books about feelings, and a game inventor. She is a licensed family life educator and leads workshops internationally on managing feelings and raising self-esteem.

Marion J. London, prevention specialist, is the training manager for Project Charlie, an international drug abuse prevention program. She has worked in the field of prevention and education for over twenty years. Marion was a contributing author of the Project Charlie curriculum and has trained over 2,500 educators in prevention throughout the world. She holds a master's degree in education.